For Jayne Loftus and Sasha

Published by The Bluecoat Press, Liverpool
Book design by March Design, Liverpool
Front cover illustration by Bronek Kram
Printed by Biddles Ltd

ISBN 1 872568 62 9

Haunted
CHESHIRE

Tom Slemen

The Bluecoat Press

Contents

Introduction

If you're looking for traditional, stereotyped ghost stories, you've come to the wrong book. You won't find any clichéd, chain-rattling ghosts roaming castle ruins among these pages, nor will you encounter any of the regurgitated Cheshire legends which pad out so many books on supernatural folklore. Within this volume I have culled a fascinating and thought-provoking collection of stories from my extensive files on the paranormal. During the research for my previous books on the ghosts of Merseyside, which resulted in the Haunted Liverpool Series, I accumulated a wealth of material concerning the county of Cheshire. Most of the stories came from Cheshire people who heard me guesting on several phone-in programmes on Magic 1548, a Liverpool radio station, which broadcasts to Merseyside, Cheshire, Lancashire and North Wales. By telephone, letters, faxes and e-mail, Cheshire listeners bombarded me with intriguing tales of ghostly hitch-hikers, doppelgangers, curses, angels, time-warps, phone calls from the deceased, banshees, vampires and spine-chilling premonitions. The response was phenomenal and quite unexpected.

Ghosts feature in most of the stories covered in this book but what are they? In most people's minds, ghosts are assumed to be visitors from a supernatural realm. Statisticians say that around 1 in 5 people now believe in ghosts and roughly 1 in 10 claim to have seen one.

From my own research over the years, I would say that there are several common myths about ghosts. They don't always put in an appearance after dark and are often encountered in broad daylight, sometimes looking as solid as you and I. One clear giveaway is their outdated attire but phantoms of the recently-departed usually wear contemporary clothes. The shroud-draped shade is simply a corny caricature.

Another myth is that ghosts are harmless, yet poltergeists have seriously injured many people by hurling objects at them and lifting them bodily into the air. Many years ago, a Londoner was thrown out of a second floor window by a poltergeist and almost broke his neck. Poltergeists have also caused fires and may be the cause of the occasional blazes which arson investigators can't explain.

The sudden appearance of a ghost can cause traumatic shock and may even trigger cardiac arrest in susceptible individuals. So ghosts can physically harm you, although most spectres are benign.

There are roughly six types of ghost:

1) Carnate; a solid-looking entity which you can touch. This type of ghost usually interacts with witnesses.

2) Discarnate; an entity which has no physical body. It usually makes its presence known by a drop in temperature. Poltergeists are always discarnate and some ghosts of this type have never lived previously in a physical state.

3) Psychological; these 'ghosts' are hallucinations which appear to one person for various subjective reasons: hypnagogic (border of sleep) visions, optical illusions, drugs, drink, schizophrenia, etc.

4) Doppelgangers; phantasms of the living which are projected images of a living person, who is usually ill or experiencing an emotional crisis.

5) Re-enacting ghosts; these are carnate or semi-transparent images of people, animals or inanimate objects which appear to be limited in their actions and repeatedly re-enact a specific scene. The cause may be something to do with the nature of time itself (technically called time hysteresis by physicists).

6) Extra-dimensional; these are entities which are thought to originate outside our space-time continuum and may include visitors from the future.

Belief in ghosts is not confined to one particular culture or class. They have been reported for thousands of years by people of every creed and caste. Even the royals have reported ghostly encounters. Prince Charles – who has an avid interest in the paranormal – is said to have seen the ghost of Henry VIII at Hampton Court in the 1970s. Her Majesty the Queen, Prince Phillip and the Queen Mother have allegedly attended many seances over the years to communicate with King George VI, who died in 1952. In May 1997, Prince Edward and a film crew spotted a phantom galleon while filming the second episode of his 'Queen and Country' TV series on the Isle of Wight. Edward was telling the story of HMS Eurydice, a 26 gun frigate which capsized and sank in Sandown Bay in 1878, when one of the film crew shouted:

'Look! There's one now!'

The ghostly image of a three-masted schooner suddenly started to materialise on the horizon in broad daylight. After five minutes, the mystery ship vanished as eerily as it had appeared but, incredibly, it was all captured on camera, which ruled out a collective hallucination. The unique footage was later shown on television and video experts who analysed the tape ruled out camera trickery. Prince Edward later told the press,

'I am quite convinced, as far as ghosts are concerned, that there are too many stories, coincidences, occurrences and strange happenings. There is something definitely out there, but what it is I don't really know.'

Ironically, physics has now reached an uneasy point where it has been established that all objects in the universe, including ourselves, are but 'ripples of energy in the quantum field'. This means, in essence, that we are all ghosts of a sort, as the atoms which make up our very bodies and consciousness, are but flickering particles of energy which can never be clearly analysed. Quantum physics has therefore ascertained that our personal atoms are merely as real as starlight or a radio wave. The English quantum physicist, Sir James Jeans, once mystically remarked that 'the stuff of the universe is mind stuff'. Perhaps he was referring, in layman's terms, to the phantom-like nature of matter at the sub-atomic level. Another renowned physicist, Sir Arthur Eddington, also once commented, that 'the whole universe functions like a great thought'. In 'The Tempest', Shakespeare makes a similar conjecture about the ultimate flimsy nature of reality:

'These our actors, as I foretold you, were all spirits and are melted into air... We are such stuff as dreams are made on, and our little life is rounded with a sleep.'

I am often asked by my readers if I believe in an afterlife – I do – I think we go on to a dimension of the mind and end up on some other plane of existence. I suspect that many spirits return to the environment of their old life because of unfinished business; perhaps because they love someone so intensely that they cannot wait until that person comes over to join them. I can imagine a caring parent returning to oversee his or her children as they grow up. One of the most convincing cases of an afterlife is the so-called 'Cross-correspondences' case, which took place over a thirty year period. After the deaths of several founder members of the Society of Psychical Research (SPR), most notably that of FWH Myers, fragmentary messages were picked up all over the world by different mediums. When these seemingly nonsensical messages – written in Greek, Latin and complex anagrams – were ultimately compiled over 30 years, they spelt out what amounted to a declaration from the dead SPR founders, that they were alive and well in the afterlife. As the Edwardian era came to a close to give way to 20th century scepticism, the messages from Myers and his colleagues stopped. It seems that communications only ceased because mediumship was soon ridiculed in classically-educated, upper-middle-class circles. Those with a gift for automatic writing were similarly derided, so perhaps Myers was still transmitting his messages but there was no one on his wavelength to receive and transcribe them. However, in 1972, a gifted English psychic, Matthew Manning, received an intriguing automatic script, signed by F Myers, which read:

'You should not indulge in this unless you know what you are doing. I did a lot of work on automatic writing when I was alive and I could never work it out. No one alive will ever work out the whole secret of life after death. It pivots on so many things – personality – condition of the mental and physical bodies. Carry on trying though, because you could soon be close to the secret. If you find it, no one else will believe you anyway.'

As ever, I leave it to the reader to make up his or her own mind. One thing is certain, however; one day you will find out from first-hand experience what happens at death.

Tom Slemen

The haunted roads of Cheshire

If the following collection of spooky tales is to be believed, the highways and byways of Cheshire have their ghosts. In all of the thought-provoking accounts I am about to relate, there is one common denominator; the apparent solidity of the apparitions, which are often seen by more than one witness.

One sultry summer night in July 1983, a 42-year-old hairdresser named Gareth, set out from Northwich on his 250cc Honda motorcycle and headed for his girlfriend's home in Frodsham. He was travelling along the B5153, with which he was very familiar, as he had been making the journey three or four times a week for a couple of months. On this particular night, the full moon was suspended in a cloudless sky, illuminating the fields and the long winding road ahead.

As Gareth sped past the village of Crowton, he happened to glance at the luminous dial of his analogue wristwatch and noticed that it was midnight. He looked up and saw the silhouette of a person standing at the side of the road up ahead, about half a mile away. He slowed slightly and cautiously approached the shadowy figure, wondering if it was a decoy for a roadside mugging. But as he got nearer, he realised it was a woman and she was waving and gesticulating for him to stop.

Gareth decided to pull over but he looked about suspiciously, in case the woman had associates lying in wait. But the girl was alone and she ran over to him smiling broadly. She had long, straight, black hair and an attractive, pale round face. She was unusually tall, possibly over six foot and, although it was a sweltering summer night, she wore a long dark overcoat.

'Thanks for stopping,' she said, standing in front of the motorbike. She didn't speak with a local accent at all but in a cultivated, urbane sort of voice, almost aristocratic. The stranger then asked Gareth if he was going to Helsby. He said he wasn't but offered to give her a lift as far as the fork in the road beyond Kingsley. She nodded and, with a grateful expression, clasped her hands together as if in prayer and closed her eyes.

'What are you doing out here on your own, anyway?' Gareth asked, as he offered her the spare crash helmet he'd unfastened from the rear seat. The girl pushed the helmet down on her head,

'Oh, I lost my way.' She didn't elaborate but mounted the pillion seat and threw her arms around Gareth's waist.

The hairdresser proceeded to the fork in the road just beyond Kingsley. Then something eerie happened. Gareth was suddenly aware that the girl's arms were no longer gripping his waist. He stopped and turned around. The pillion seat was empty, the helmet attached to its usual space. Gareth was understandably baffled and a little frightened by the hitch-hiker's sudden disappearance. As he tried to rationalise the bizarre incident, he noticed a light in his wing mirror, which turned out to be a police car. A policeman wound down the window and politely asked if everything was okay. Gareth didn't know what to say because he doubted that the police, or anyone for that matter, would believe his strange tale. After an uncomfortable pause, he finally admitted,

'I gave a girl a lift and the next minute she's not there.'

The two policemen looked at each other knowingly,

'Did you pick her up near Crowton, by any chance?'

'Yeah, why?'

'We've had a few reports of a phantom hitch-hiker along here over the years. You saw her once didn't you?'

The other policeman nodded and turned to Gareth,

'Did she ask to be dropped off at Helsby?'

'Yeah, she did. What do you mean, phantom hitch-hiker?'

'Erm, let's leave it at that. More things in heaven and earth and all that,' The policeman averted his gaze, wound up his window and focused on the road ahead.

'What do you mean? Who is she?' Gareth's voice fell on deaf ears. The driver merely flashed his headlights, before continuing down the moonlit road.

Gareth didn't hang around and he sped off to his girlfriend's house. The hairdresser later learnt from several people in Frodsham that the ghostly hitch-hiking girl is often seen standing at the side of the road near Crowton on nights when the moon is full. No one seems to know who she is, or was, which adds an extra dimension of mystery to the solid-looking apparition.

Not all phantoms of the road are as innocuous as the Crowton hitch-hiker; some are nothing short of terrifying, as a young Wilmslow man discovered one winter's evening in 1991. In January of that year, a 20-year-old student named Craig was cycling down a secluded country lane, bordered by hedgerows, on the outskirts of Ollerton, which lies a couple of miles to the south-east of Knutsford. The time was 9.15pm and, as Craig approached a curve in the road, he heard the clip-clop of a horse's hooves. As he rounded the bend, he was confronted with a sight that gave him nightmares for weeks. Treading the ground at the side of the road was a black horse mounted by a man in black, wearing an antiquated tricorn hat. The lower half of the horseman's pale face was covered with a scarf; in other words, he looked just like a highwayman from the 18th century.

Craig remembers frantically praying that some historical drama was being filmed but, as he sped past the ominous-looking rider, he found no film technicians or arc lights anywhere. Worse still, he could now hear the hooves pounding towards him. He panicked, changed gear and found himself literally pedalling for his life. But his modern mountain bike was no match for the galloping steed thundering down on him. He thought he heard the eerie highwayman shouting something to him but he couldn't quite make out what it was. It sounded like, 'Halt, you devil!'

Craig experienced severe palpitations when the black-clad rider and his horse drew parallel to the bike. He slammed on his brakes and the robber continued down the lane on his ebony-coloured mount.

The student abandoned his bike and ran off across a field. His legs felt like jelly but, glancing back to the road, he could see no sign of the menacing man on the horse. He walked the two miles home and, when he returned with two of his friends, he was relieved to find that his mountain bike was still where he had left it at the edge of the road. He later learned from locals in the area, that a spectral masked highwayman allegedly haunts several of the lanes on the outskirts of Knutsford. Many level-headed people had reputedly encountered him over the years at Ollerton, Marthall and Chelford.

Some claim that the ghost rider is that of 'Gentleman' Higgins, a notorious highwayman who operated around Knutsford in the mid 18th century. Higgins was a respected citizen of Knutsford by day and a ruthless brigand of Cheshire's turnpike roads and lonely country lanes after dark. Higgins started to operate much further afield and, after being caught while breaking into a house in Carmarthen, he was hanged at the gallows. From the accounts I have heard of the phantom highwayman, I would claim it is not the ghost of Higgins. All reports of the shadowy rider mention the sound of hooves, yet it is a recorded fact that Gentleman Higgins always muffled his horse's hooves with woollen socks for extra stealth, before embarking on his nocturnal ambushes. The ghost then, could be the phantasm of one of several highwaymen, who were the scourge of travellers on the roads of 18th century Cheshire.

In May 1998, I received an interesting letter from a middle-aged chap named Graham who lives in Little Neston. Graham wrote to tell me that, although he does not believe in ghosts, he is at a loss to explain the following weird incident. On a bright spring afternoon at around 2 o'clock in 1996, he was cycling out of Burton village. As he passed the village school on his way to Puddington, Graham detected the distinctive sound of another cyclist behind him. He glanced back out of curiosity and saw a man in his forties wearing a bowler hat and seated on an Edwardian-style bicycle, about twelve feet away.

Graham pulled over to let the time-displaced cyclist pass by, in order to get a better look at him, but the Edwardian gent was suddenly nowhere to be seen, yet there was no layby or lane turning off the road. He was absolutely dumbfounded and he rode back the way he had come, realising that the cyclist was not of the 20th century. His personal beliefs told him that there were no such things as ghosts, but his strange encounter suggested otherwise.

The next spooky tale unfolds at Shotwick, just a stone's throw from the area where the phantom Edwardian cyclist was seen.

One summer night in May 1995, a transit van carrying three teenagers, set off from Shotwick to a secret rendezvous over the Welsh border, where an open-air rave was to be held. 18-year-old Damon was driving his two friends Aaron and Daniel, who were both a year younger. Before the van left Cheshire, the lads were surprised to see a girl standing at the side of the road. Damon pulled up alongside her and Aaron wound down the passenger window to ask if she wanted a lift. The girl stood there motionless, the only movement caused by a light summer breeze ruffling the folds of her long, white, flowing dress. Her long blonde hair blew across her face as she smiled and nodded slightly.

The girl seemed unaffected by Aaron's impatience and calmly walked over to the open door of the transit and climbed in. At this point, Aaron and Damon noticed that she was barefooted. Daniel reluctantly vacated the middle seat and clambered into the back of the van. The girl was absolutely stunning. She had a clear-complexioned, elfin face, a little snub nose, a pair of large expressive blue eyes and perfectly shaped 'cupid's bow' lips. She looked about sixteen – eighteen at the most.

'Where do you wanna go?'

'Buckley.' The girl's timid, child-like voice was barely audible.

'Do you live there?'

The girl just nodded and gazed morosely through the windscreen as the van moved off.

'We're going to a rave. Fancy coming?'

She smiled and shrugged and, from the way she was behaving, the lads started to suspect that she was stoned on drugs. Perhaps she was just a stranded New Age traveller. Aaron introduced himself and his two mates, then asked her name.

'Hattie.'

'What music are you into, Hattie?'

'The Beatles.'

'Oh they were cool weren't they? Don't you like the Prodigy or Oasis?'

'Who are they?' The bands obviously meant nothing to her.

A couple of miles further down the road, Aaron tried to make a pass at the beautiful hitch-hiker. Noticing that she was wearing an onyx ring, he gently took hold of her hand,

'That's a lovely ring.' He was shocked to feel that Hattie's hand was literally as cold as ice.

'Let me off here,' Hattie suddenly demanded and she tried to scramble over Aaron's lap to reach the door.

'Okay, okay, hang on!' said Damon, startled by the girl's sudden lunge at the passenger door. He pulled over and they watched, disappointed, as Hattie jumped out. She slammed the door shut behind her and, without uttering a thankyou, she walked towards the back of the van.

'You ingrate!' fumed Damon.

Then something creepy happened. Daniel glanced out of the rear windows of the transit to see where Hattie was heading – but she had apparently vanished.

Damon checked his wing mirrors and Aaron even got out of the van to look for her, but it was as if she had disappeared into thin air.

The three lads were naturally unnerved by Hattie's vanishing trick and the realisation that they might have given a lift to a supernatural being slowly dawned on them. They quickly got back into the van and were soon continuing on their journey. As they were travelling down the A550 near Queensferry, Damon screamed out,

'Look!'

Aaron and Daniel scanned the road ahead, expecting to discover what had alarmed him. But Damon nodded in the rear view mirror,

'No, look behind!'

Aaron and Daniel turned in their seats and looked back. What they saw made them shudder. Hattie's face was staring through one of the reardoor windows, as if she was clinging on to the back of the vehicle. Her fluttering locks radiated out from her ghastly, pallid and expressionless face in the vehicle's slipstream.

'Oh my God!' Aaron trembled and told Damon to pull up.

Damon and Daniel were transfixed with terror. Damon went into a higher gear and accelerated, hoping he'd shake the 'thing' off from his van. A Volvo estate came alongside in the right lane and a passenger stared out with an expression of horror at the back of the transit, as if she could see the ghost too. The Volvo then sped away up the motorway.

The face vanished as mysteriously as it had appeared. The boys were so scared, they turned off the motorway and headed back home to Cheshire, no longer in the mood for raving.

I have since learnt that a number of motorists and several policemen have allegedly spotted a barefooted girl with long blonde hair who walks along the embankment near the A550 near Shotwick in the early hours. What's more, this ghost – who has been sighted in the area since the early 1970s – is seen mostly during May and June but why this is so, and who she is, or was, is still a complete mystery. Perhaps we will uncover more about her one day.

At 1.15am precisely on October 15th 1987, two barmaids from Winsford named Helen and Angela, were travelling to Crewe to visit friends. They were travelling down the A530 in Helen's mini, when they saw a woman in black standing on the hard shoulder, next to a Volkswagen beetle, which seemed to have broken down.

As Helen drew nearer to the stranger, she became aware that she was an elderly nun, so she pulled over. Angela wound down the nearside window and asked her what was wrong.

'It just packed up.'

'Have you called anyone out?'

'No, my friend only lives a mile down the road. I'll walk.' And she set off along the edge of the road.

'No, wait. We'll give you a lift.' Helen pushed forward Angela's seat to allow the nun to get into the back of the little car and Angela patiently eased the old woman into the vehicle.

'Oh thank you. You're so kind.'

Helen asked her where she wanted to be dropped off and the nun said,

'It's just a little sliproad before Willaston. You'll miss it if you blink. I'll point it out to you.'

Helen tried to make conversation by telling their passenger that they had two days off work and were going to spend them with their friends in Crewe.

'Good for you,' was the curt reply, then she lapsed into silence.

The atmosphere in the mini became increasingly claustrophobic, so

Angela asked the nun which convent she was from but received no reply. She just stared at the road ahead, leaving Helen feeling nervous. She began to wonder if the woman in the back really was a nun, or was she some psychotic impostor, who had perhaps donned the disguise to gain the girls' confidence. As her imagination got the better of her, she considered the possibility of the passenger having a knife.

After a few minutes of this stifling silence, the nun suddenly declared,

'There's a terrible storm on the way. It's going to kill people and do a lot of damage.'

'Really?' said Angela, immensely relieved that the passenger was talking at last.

Helen had heard the national and local weather forecasts before setting out and there hadn't been any mention of a storm, so she thought the nun's comments were unfounded. After her brief outburst, the nun resumed her silence. When they came to a roadsign indicating that Willaston was just a few miles ahead, Helen asked,

'Are we near the turn-off yet?'

Simultaneously, Angela let out a scream.

'What's wrong?'

'She's gone!'

Helen pulled over and confirmed for herself that her friend was right. The backseat was completely bare. The nun had inexplicably vanished; the only clue to her ever having been there was a faint but unmistakable smell of incense.

On arrival at their friends' house in Crewe, they told them of the terrifying encounter with the phantom nun. The barmaids sat up for the remainder of the night drinking coffee and repeatedly going over the details of the creepy encounter. They told their friends about the nun's curious warning about a terrible storm and ensuing loss of life. Their friends were sceptical at first but could see that something had made the barmaids very anxious and jumpy. Later that morning, Angela telephoned the police and recounted the details of their experience. The police were naturally amused but promised to check if there was an abandoned Volkswagen beetle on the hard shoulder of the A530. They phoned her back a few hours later to say that there was no sign of a beetle car and nor had the AA or RAC been called out to repair or tow away such a vehicle.

Of course, later that day, weather forecasters failed, right up to the last moment, to predict the arrival of Britain's worst storm in two centuries. A hurricane swept across the country, uprooting nineteen million trees, killing nineteen people, and causing £1.5 billion worth of damage. Strangely enough, there was another uncanny warning about the approaching hurricane which went unheeded. BBC weatherman, Michael Fish, calmly told millions of viewers that he had just received a frantic telephone call from an anonymous woman warning that a hurricane was approaching the UK. Fish smugly discredited the woman's claim and asserted that no such storm was posing a threat.

Who was the nun who prophesied the storm? My own research has drawn a blank but, curiously enough, in April 1980, scores of motorists in the north-western American states of Washington and Oregon reported picking up a nun, stranded on the highway, who subsequently warned them of a volcano that was about to erupt in the USA. On 18th May, Mount St Helens, in south-west Washington, erupted with enormous violence, causing widespread destruction and 50 deaths.

In October 1979, a retired doctor, Alan Harris, was driving home to Hale in Cheshire from Warrington. The time was 11pm and, as he was driving his Ford Cortina down a B road near the A56, the figure of a small child appeared in his headlights. The Cortina hit the child at 60mph and threw her up into the air. Dr Harris screeched to a halt, then jumped out of his vehicle and inspected the tarmac with a mounting sense of dread. The broken body of a little girl with long black hair, lay motionless at the side of the road. Harris fetched a blanket from the back seat of his car and wrapped her in it. He knew he wasn't supposed to move the victim but he was in shock and, thinking the child was dead, he panicked and chanced taking her to the nearest hospital.

Harris placed the limp little body on the back seat of his car and drove like a madman to the nearest hospital. As he screeched into the car park, he turned round and, where the child had lain, there was only the blanket which had cocooned her. Still convinced there had been an accident, he drove to a police station near Bowdon and gave a statement but, after the police had looked into the matter, the desk sergeant reassured Harris that the light played very funny tricks on the stretch of road near Dunham Massey. Harris insisted that what had occurred had not been some optical illusion but the police simply advised him to have a coffee before continuing his journey home. Dr Harris learned many years later that numerous motorists had apparently run down a phantom girl, who later melted away. No one knows her identity and she is still occasionally spotted on the same motorway.

Another mystery of the macadam took place one sunny Saturday in July 1994, when Mr and Mrs Carbury, a retired couple from Chester, set out on a 40 mile journey to Buxton in their Ford Orion. Mr Carbury took a wrong turning at some point on the A54 after Congleton and lost his bearings. His wife added to his embarrassment by sighing impatiently as she put on her specs to consult the road atlas. Mr Carbury searched desperately for some road sign to tell him just where he was. He finally pulled up halfway down a quiet lane and was trying to wrestle the atlas from his wife, when someone tapped on the nearside window, making the quarrelling couple jump with fright. They turned to see a man of around eighty with white, swept-back hair. When asked to describe the stranger, the Carburys both agreed that he had the same face as the man on the Quaker Oats box! Despite his age, he had a jovial, rosy-cheeked face with a pair of lively, smiling eyes.

The old man glanced at the atlas on Mrs Carbury's lap and chuckled.

'I take it you're lost then?'

Mrs Carbury said they were looking for Buxton and the stranger gave them detailed directions which were so comprehensive that Mr Carbury had to jot them down.

The man then walked off as the Carburys thanked him and, without turning, he raised his right hand and gave a little wave of acknowledgement. He wore a white shirt, grubby-looking jeans with braces, and a pair of wellington boots. Then something weird happened. As Mr Carbury slowly reversed out of the lane, he glanced in his rear-view mirror and could detect no trace of the helpful old man. He had literally vanished. His sudden disappearance naturally made them uneasy and they were only too glad to leave that silent lane. But the strange episode does not end there. Minutes later, ten miles further up the A54, near Allgreave, Mr Carbury was pulling into a service station for refreshments, when his wife spotted the old man walking across a field. Both of them were baffled as to how he had travelled up the motorway, presumably on foot, before them.

After a brief stop at the service station, they resumed their journey to Buxton. For a couple of hours they enjoyed their tour of the famous spa, Poole's Cavern, Solomon's Temple and various other tourist sights, before embarking on the journey back to Chester. But the Cestrians were in for a shock. As the afternoon progressed, the A54 became quite congested with weekend traffic, so Mr Carbury decided to find an alternative route out of the jam. This resulted in him losing his way again, ten minutes after leaving the motorway. A roadsign told him he was near a place with the quaint name of Wildboarclough. Mrs Carbury urged her husband to stop the vehicle and ask one of the locals for directions but Mr Carbury insisted that he knew the general direction and stubbornly refused to stop. Twenty minutes later, the Carbury's Ford Orion was travelling towards Macclesfield, when Mrs Carbury again consulted the road atlas.

'You idiot,' she seethed, 'you're going in the wrong direction. You're going north instead of west.'

'Things look different on a map; just be quiet.'

Mr Carbury then realised that his wife was right and that, if he proceeded on his present course, he'd end up on the A537. He finally stopped, intending to do a U-turn, when he again caught sight of the old man. He was sitting on a low, crumbling stone wall which bordered the field adjacent to the road. As Mr Carbury pulled up, the old man smiled,

'Lost again? You two need a compass.'

He walked over to the Orion and asked the startled couple where they wanted to get to this time. Mrs Carbury was so shocked at seeing the mysterious old man once more, that she could barely stammer out a reply.

'Erm, Chester.'

Once again, they were given elaborate directions, which Mr Carbury scribbled down and, before driving off, he said to the old man,

'You certainly get around don't you?'

The obliging stranger simply winked and smiled enigmatically without uttering a word.

The couple still occasionally journey to the Peak District, not only to enjoy the splendour of the high peat moorlands and towering limestone crags, but also to see if they can once again meet up with the mysterious old man whom they regard as some guiding angel to the lost.

Well, what are we to make of these ghosts of the road? As anyone who has driven alone at night knows, even on the most familiar well-lit road or motorway, the mind gets lulled into a trance-like state of disassociation – especially if you are fatigued. as the road scrolls hypnotically towards the moving vehicle, the change in the driver's state of mind possibly makes him or her more susceptible to hallucinations from the fertile subconscious. But how would such a theory explain some of the aforementioned cases, where more than one person witnessed a hitch-hiking or roadside ghost? What's more, the figure the Carburys met appeared in daylight. My personal view is that most of the phenomena haunting the roads of our counties are real and not subjective mirages. The subconscious really is the last refuge of the cornered sceptic, when rational explanations are desperately sought.

Whether the previously-mentioned entities are the earthbound spirits of automobile tragedies, is difficult to establish. I leave it up to you to make up your own mind.

Infernal tales

The Cheshire town of Nantwich lies just a few miles to the south-west of Crewe and the following two short tales, which occurred within the town's vicinity, both have one thing in common, fire, the devil's best friend.

On the evening of Monday 9th December 1583, the townsfolk of Nantwich witnessed a most peculiar and bemusing sight: an exodus of cats. A long file of some thirty or more of them calmly pussyfooted their way from Nantwich High Street. The cats strolled intently from every alleyway and hiding hole in the thoroughfare and not even several infuriated dogs could dissuade the cheeky column from slinking out of the town centre. Men, women and children laughed and pointed at the trail of cats and some bystanders attempted to break up the line, but the cats seemed impervious to their disruptive efforts and marched on as if they were in some hypnotic trance.

During the week preceding the bizarre spectacle, the local people had noticed that a large number of the town's cats had gone astray, but most cat owners never suspected anything sinister. Nor did any of the Nantwich folk give any further thought to the feline parade, as it disappeared into the night. With historical hindsight, it looks as if the old adage 'animals have more sense' is true, for, on the day following the exodus, a blaze erupted in Nantwich which was to take a devastating toll. At 4.15pm, a fire broke out in the kitchen of a house in the High Street which rapidly spread through the thatched, wooden-beamed dwelling. Strong winds fanned the flames and glowing sparks eastwards and, within seconds, the house next door was also alight. The gale-driven inferno acted like a gigantic blowtorch, incinerating the adjoining tinder-dry houses down the entire length of the street. Mass panic broke out as the street became engulfed in flames and choking black clouds of smoke. People fled their homes and others suffered disfiguring burns trying to retrieve their belongings. Some brave souls died while attempting to save their properties by hurling buckets of water at the ravenous fire. Others were charred to ash as they desperately tried to stem the blaze by pulling the burning thatch to the ground with so-called firehooks. The first gruesome death was that of Mrs Anne Lovatt, who was part of a human chain passing buckets of water from the river. The wall of a gutted house toppled onto her and literally flattened the unfortunate woman. The next death was quite bizarre. A young woman named Maggie Duckworth, half-blinded by the acrid smoke, found herself confronted by four enormous bears, which lumbered out of the stifling clouds. They had been released by the landlord of the Bear Inn, where they had been kept as a cruel novelty. Upon seeing the confused and terrified bears, Maggie turned on her heels and ran off screaming. Her blackened skeleton was later discovered among the debris. The roasted corpse of a decrepit old widow named Alice Blagge was also found in the ashes of the fire, which burned for fifteen hours, destroying 150 houses and 7 inns. By a strange quirk of fate, St Mary's Church was spared, so that many in Nantwich concluded that the fire had been God's warning to the townsfolk to behave themselves.

When news of the terrible fire reached Queen Elizabeth I, she immediately arranged for a national collection to be taken for the rebuilding of Nantwich and she also diverted over £1,000 from government funds to the fire-ravaged town. The Queen also decreed that wood was to be taken from the trees of Delamere Forest for the reconstruction of the town. Only months after the great fire did some of the inhabitants of Nantwich notice the curious mass return of the missing cats.

In the western suburbs of Nantwich, near to the banks of the Shropshire Union Canal, another strange incident was reported in 1959. One foggy evening in the December of that year, a 29-year-old Wrexham man, Alan Hughes, was visiting his cousins in Nantwich. He left the house of one cousin near Acton and walked almost a mile to the home of his other cousin, George Kinsey, on a farmstead on the western periphery of Nantwich. He had never visited George before and because of the fog he gradually lost his bearings. He met an old man who helpfully directed him to follow a lane which would lead him to his destination.

Night fell fast as he made his way down the quiet lane and he was relieved to see a rosy halo of light in the distance. At first, he assumed it to be the lights of his cousin's house but he soon realised that it was a fire. Alan assumed the worst and prayed that it wasn't his cousin's house that was ablaze. He ran towards the crackling fire and as he drew near to it, he could smell the pungent fumes drifting from the blaze.

A solitary silhouette stood dangerously near to the blazing building. As Alan drew nearer, he made out a woman wearing a shawl, who turned and screamed to him,

'My baby is in there! Please save him!'

Alan hesitated for a moment to regain his breath, coughing as the acrid smoke wafted towards him but the woman screeched at him again,

'Please! Save my baby! He's upstairs!' She then backed away from the squat granite dwelling, which looked like a farmhouse or lodge of some sort.

He looked apprehensively at the thick smoke billowing from the doorway, then took a huge breath and rushed in. He fought through the smokey blackness, until he tripped over what seemed to be a step. He attempted to feel his way up the staircase but the heat and suffocating smoke forced him back out into the open. When he emerged, the woman was nowhere to be seen and Alan felt dizzy from smoke inhalation. He fell to his knees, unable to expel the asphyxiating soot from his lungs, then passed out.

When he came to, he found himself in an open field. The fog had evaporated and, by the light of a waning moon on the eastern horizon, he could see that no buildings or landmarks of any kind were visible. He felt a bit groggy but his lungs were fine. He searched the field, determind to find the burnt-out house but, like the fog, it had apparently vanished into thin air. By the time Alan finally found his cousin's house, it was 3am and he quickly realised that it bore no resemblance whatsoever to the one that had been on fire.

However, on the following day in the local inn, Alan and his cousin were enjoying a drink as they discussed the strange incident of the previous night, when the old landlady leaned over to them. She said she had been listening to their conversation and that over a hundred years ago, a cottage had been razed by a fire which killed the baby son of a farmer. The farmer had been visiting his mistress at the time of the blaze and many suspected that he had deliberately started it to rid himself of his wife because he claimed her newborn son wasn't his. The farmer's wife attempted to save her baby boy from the flames but was driven back by the heat and smoke and the baby perished. The landlady added that over the years, several people had seen the phantom fire while crossing the field where the cottage had once stood.

Cheshire timewarps

In the relatively short span we spend on earth, one thing above all rules our lives: time. Even the richest man in the world lying on his deathbed, cannot buy one extra second of time. Time is more precious than gold but cannot be borrowed or bought, although we often talk of someone buying time or living on borrowed time. These are just misleading idioms. As Paul Henri Spaak, the Belgian statesman once wistfully remarked, on the almost cruel ephemerality of fleeting time:

'If an hour seems long, I remind myself that it will never return and it immediately becomes terribly short.'

But what is time? Does it really have something to do with the clocks and watches which dictate our lives, or is it all in the mind? We all know that if you're having an unpleasant experience, time drags by, but if you're enjoying yourself, the hours fly; it's as if time were a subjective experience. Neurologists now claim that the brain's complex architecture may be partly responsible for our experience of personal time. If you have a personal computer nowadays, the manufacturer often states how fast the PC is by quoting the speed of its processor, which is usually measured in megahertz (MHz). One megahertz is a measure of frequency equal to one million cycles per second. Personal computers have a component containing a quartz crystal which vibrates millions of times per second and acts as the heart of a clock for the computer system to work by. Most computers have a processor speed of 200 MHz but, believe it or not, the human brain – the most complex computer known to man – has a much slower frequency of just 18 Hz – or eighteen cycles per second. The eminent neurologist, J Hughlings Jackson, recently stated that,

'Time, in the form of some minimum duration, is required for consciousness.'

Many other prominent neurologists concur and believe that psychological time – our experience of the present – is merely an illusory side-effect, created by the ticking of the brain's electrical 18

Hz clock. This would mean that the ego of the reader only exists in relatively slow measurable pulses of 18 cycles per second. In other words, the ego is discontinuous, like a number of beads spaced out on a thread. Curiously, the Buddhists have long asserted that the ego is a flickering, virtually non-existent illusion of continuity. A good analogy to illustrate this concept of discontinuity, is the way in which we are fooled into believing we are watching a continuous 'motion' film in the cinema, when we are actually only looking at 24 still frames per second, being swiftly flashed onto the screen in succession. The audience experiences a sense of 'now' unfolding each moment in the film's time frame when, in reality, it is just a discontinuous illusion, full of blank gaps and static images.

The clock theory of the brain would also explain why certain people suffer convulsions and seizures when they are bombarded with rapid flashes of light from a strobe. Most of the seizures take place when the strobe flashes at a frequency of 15 to 20 Hz. It is as if the flashes are sending high-speed signals down the eye's optic nerve, which throw the brain out of synchronization with its 18 Hz rhythm, just like a drummer losing his beat. Despite these intriguing mechanistic theories of consciousness, I still suspect that the neurologists are grossly underestimating the complex workings of the psyche and are merely skirting the fringes of the human mindscape.

So much for psychological time. Does time exist outside our brains in the physical universe? The Greek philosopher Heraclitus (c540-c480 BC) was one of the earliest people to ponder the nature of time and he observed that,

'All things flow, nothing stays still; nothing endures but change.'

Heraclitus was remarking on the apparent constant 'arrow of time' which travels relentlessly into the future from the past, in one direction. Empires rise and crumble, the baby grows into an old person and expires and the eternal seasons roll on. In the midst of this ever-changing universe, the nostalgic animal, homo sapiens, longs to turn back the clock to the familiar golden days of yesteryear. The receding out-of-reach past, which rouses Shakespeare's Richard II to cry,

'O! Call back yesterday, bid time return.'

Thanks to the development of photography, film and video technology, we can call back yesterday in limited form. We can re-visit a wedding captured years ago on video, be enthralled by films starring actors and actresses who have been dead for decades and listen to tapes and CDs featuring performers who have long since died. And, of course, leafing through the simple family photograph album never fails to evoke some emotion or memory of days gone by.

But can we somehow circumvent the seemingly cast-iron laws of nature and actually visit the past (or the future for that matter) in person? This seductive notion has occupied minds for thousands of years. We are now venturing into the territory of the theoretical physicist, because we are posing the age-old question: is time-travel possible? I say it is.

We are all time travellers, moving into the future at a rate of sixty seconds a minute, although we often think that it is time that is going by. No, time stays, we move on. As each second passes, the earth is whizzing through space in its orbit around the sun at a phenomenal speed of eighteen miles per second but no one is aware of this. Nor are most people aware that when they look at the setting sun, they are seeing it, not as it is now, but as it was eight minutes ago. The rays which travel from the sun across 93 million miles of space, take eight minutes to reach earth.

Of course, the sun is the nearest star to us and the light from the other stars can take anything from 4 years, to billions of years, to reach us. For example, if you go out on a cloudless night and look up at the North Star, Polaris, your eyes will be seeing it as it was 680 years ago, when Edward II was king of England. And, if by some remote chance there are aliens peering at us through their version of a super-Hubble telescope, on some planet orbiting a star 932 light years away, they will be witnessing the Battle of Hastings. Sadly, if the extra-terrestrials take another look at us 900 years on, they will still see conflicts going on down here.

So, just by gazing at the stars we can look into the remote past, which illustrates how our perspective on time changes when we look at it from beyond the confines of our mundane world of clockwatching. But observing the stars is hardly physical time travel. Isn't there a nuts and bolts way of visiting the past down here on earth? The surprising answer is yes.

Viewers of all ages have been terrified by Dr Who with his grisly gallery of outlandish monsters (and low-budget egg-box sets). The doctor and his Tardis were once regarded as pure science fiction but there are many distinguished scientists, with impeccable academic credentials, who believe that time travel will be a reality one day. Indeed, some boffins think timelords, like Dr Who, may have already visited history. Before I examine the blueprints for hypothetical time machines, let me mention one curious character of the 18th century who may have been a real-life timelord: the mysterious Count of St Germain. Various books refer to this enigmatic, aristocratic-looking individual as nothing more than some oddball adventurer. In the Century of Enlightenment, the French police suspected him of being a Prussian spy, but the Prussians surmised he was a Russian agent. The English thought he was a Jacobite sympathiser when he was arrested in London in 1745 but, whenever he was interrogated, it became clear that the Count was not in the pay of anybody and made many disturbing and seemingly astounding claims.

He insisted he had met Jesus of Nazareth and had been a wedding guest at Cana, where he actually witnessed the water-into-wine miracle. He added that he had always known that Christ would meet a bad end and many were outraged by his sacrilegious claims. The Count said he had also met Cleopatra, Nefertiti, Henry VIII, Shakespeare and many other historical characters. Stranger still, when quizzed by bemused historians about his meetings with celebrated people from the past, he always went into amazing detail about his encounters and could even describe the food, weather and trivialities of the age he had lived in. All these details were thoroughly checked by the academics and were always found to be true.

Another mystery was the Count's wealth. He was incredibly rich, with an abundant supply of unusually large gemstones, which he used as currency. Then there is the puzzle of his multi-linguistic talents. He spoke fluent Greek, Spanish, Russian, Italian, Portugese, French, Arabic, Sanskrit, Chinese, English and the language of Christ – Aramaic. The Count was also a gifted violinist, pianist, sculptor (in the ancient Greek tradition), painter, and an accomplished chemist. He set up many laboratories during his extensive travels throughout Europe, Russia and India but his work was always shrouded in secrecy, although many thought he was an alchemist trying to turn base metals into gold.

The great French writer and philosopher, Voltaire, quizzed the Count, initially suspecting him to be a silver-tongued charlatan but ending up declaring,

'He is truly a man who never dies and knows so much.'

But the greatest conundrum concerning the Count of St Germain is his incredible longevity. According to reliable eye-witness reports and the numerous entries in aristrocrats' diaries, the Count appeared to be 45 to 50 years of age in 1710, yet he is known to have been active in the French Revolution of 1789. In fact, he was even mentioned in the diary of Marie Antoinette, who recorded her regret at not taking the advice of the 'Comte de St Germain, as he had long ago warned of the gigantic conspiracy which would overthrow the order of things'. During the Reign of Terror in France, the unfathomable nobleman from nowhere, still looked no older than 50. The last reliable documented sighting of him took place in 1821, 111 years after he appeared on the European scene, and the Count still looked like a 50-year-old man. Shortly before he vanished from the continent, he told a writer named Franz Graeffer,

'Tomorrow night I am off; I am much needed in Constantinople, then in England, there to prepare two inventions which you will have in the next century – trains and steamboats.'

After his arrival in England, the Count of St Germain travelled north and there were several reports of him collaborating with the engineers and promoters of the early Liverpool to Manchester railway. There were even sightings of him in Cheshire around 1829.

The only document that can be attributed to the Count is now kept in the Library at Troyes. It contains strange, apparently symbolic diagrams and a baffling text. One paragraph reads:

'We moved through space at a speed that can be compared with nothing but itself. Within a fraction of a second, the plains below us were out of sight and the earth had become a faint nebula. I was carried up, and I travelled through the empyrean for an incalculable time at an immeasurable height. Heavenly bodies revolved and worlds vanished below me.'

The Count of St Germain's lifespan seems incredible to us today, when the average expectation of life is 70. How much more phenomenal it must have seemed in the 18th century, when reaching 35 was an achievement. The Count's true identity will probably never be known, but I have a sneaking suspicion that he was a traveller in the realm of time and may have really met Jesus and Henry VIII. If he was a timelord, what sort of technology would have allowed his trek through history?

At the moment, there are two spheres of modern science which might allow a limited form of time travel: subatomic physics and cosmology. The world of subatomic particles is a topsy-turvy one which would have delighted Lewis Carroll. In the surreal, inner space universe of positrons, quarks and electrons, a ray of light consists of photons which, paradoxically, act as particles and waves. There are also elementary particles called muons which are incredibly short-lived and unstable. After 2.2 microseconds, the muon decays into an electron, neutrino and anti-neutrino. However, if the muon is pushed towards the speed of light in a particle accelerator, its lifetime is stretched a little. Travelling at 0.99% of light's speed, the muon's life is extended from a couple of microseconds to 155 microseconds. This strange effect is known as time dilation and was predicted by Einstein's Special Theory of Relativity (published in 1905). Time dilation not only stretches the lifetime of a particle, it can also extend the lifetime of a human, although the energy output and technology to achieve this would present engineering with difficulties at this moment in time.

To illustrate the weird world of time dilation, consider the following example, which was forseen by Einstein before space travel was a reality. Picture 25-year-old identical twins named Jack and Joe. Joe stays on Earth and Jack embarks on a five year tour of outer space in a rocket that travels close to the speed of light. When Jack returns to his home planet, he is five years older but Joe is 75 years old, because 50 years have elapsed on Earth since Jack set out on his journey. People accustomed to relying on commonsense down here on Earth, are puzzled by this twin brother paradox, but it is totally in accordance with relativity. Atomic clocks have been carried on Concorde and, at the end of their journey, the clocks have been compared with synchronized, high-precision timepieces left on the ground. The results are always the same; the clocks moving on Concorde ticked slower than their stationary counterparts.

Building a rocket that travels near the speed of light is not a realistic option to propel a person into another time. In fact, time dilation can only send the traveller into the future. To travel into the past would appear a trifle trickier to achieve. The universe we are familiar with is made up of 'tardyons' – particles that travel slower than the speed of light. But for some time now, scientists have been speculating upon the existence of an intriguing particle they have dubbed the 'tachyon' – a subatomic particle that travels faster than light. The tachyon only exists in theory at the moment but there is mounting evidence that it is at large in the universe. Tachyons, because of their incredible velocities, travel backwards in time and seem to fly in the face of terrestrial commonsense. An encounter with a spacecraft made of tachyons would play havoc with our sense of reality. We would see it in our vicinity first, then the spacecraft's slower light image would catch up some time later, so that we would perceive the tachyon ship as moving backwards in time and could subsequently witness its launch! This would not be some weird optical illusion but the effect of tachyonic dynamics as predicted by the Theory of Relativity.

Should scientists of the future discover a way to convert the hull of a spaceship or time machine into tachyons, the door to the past would be open and the long-held dream of returning to yesterday would become a reality. Unfortunately, the military and intelligence forces of any country would regard a time machine as a threat to national and global security. And they would have a point. Imagine some future Hitler, in the 22nd century, abusing time travel to alter the past; perhaps to massacre his adversaries' ancestors.

For all we know, these assassins from the future could already be at work in history, carrying out murders which would seem motiveless to us, yet have far-reaching influences in the politics of the future. Would this chilling possibility explain why certain people, who are always alone, have been struck down by an incredible energy force which has literally reduced them to ashes? I am referring to the hundreds of recorded deaths from so-called spontaneous human combustion, where victims have been charred to death, sometimes within seconds, often leaving their clothes and surroundings unscorched. Cremating a human body requires a considerable amount of heat. In the crematorium a temperature of 2,500-3,000 degrees Fahrenheit is required for up to four hours. But the majority of the people who die from spontaneous combustion are incinerated to powder in minutes or seconds and the fierce burning is usually so localized that a victim can be seated on a chair which remains untouched by the heat.

Then there is the sinister disturbance in the earth's magnetic field which precipitates the lethal, self-contained inferno. Each day, observatories from all over the world record readings of the earth's magnetic field. Researchers have discovered that in many areas where people have turned into human incendiary bombs, something has disturbed the magnetic field of the earth, making it more intense. The sun's solar activity was initially blamed but the real source of the disturbance remains elusive and seemingly impossible to pin down. It is as if something comes through from out of the blue to strike down the unsuspecting and apparently well-targeted victim, with an unimaginable burst of powerful, yet containable energy. Could that energy be the beam of some deadly tachyonic laser-device of the future, aimed through a tiny aperture in the space-time fabric? Is this just all paranoia – or could someone up the timeline be targeting you soon?

Getting back to the physics of time travel; most physicists have now accepted that black holes are a reality and exist in our own galaxy. A black hole is created when a massive object, such as a star, collapses in on itself, resulting in a highly-compressed sphere of super-condensed matter. The gravity is also condensed in the collapsed star and is concentrated to such an extent that even light cannot escape from it; hence it is known as a black hole. Einstein taught us that space and time are inseparable, so a hole in time is a hole in space and a whole new generation of theorists now believe that black holes are gateways to the past and future. However, a static black hole is to be avoided. Time-travellers entering black holes that do not spin, would be simply crushed out of existence at their central point – a nightmarish point of super-condensed time and space called a singularity, where the laws of physics break down.

A rotating black hole is more hospitable and offers an incredible option: travel into the remote past and future of the universe. These amazing possibilities are not pipe dreams; all the equations have been worked out and put to the test in computer simulations; all we need is a rotating black hole, but finding one near enough in the interstellar neighbourhood is a daunting problem. Locating a black hole is fairly easy, as they are usually pulling apart other stars and, as the stellar material goes down the event horizon plughole at an incredible velocity, massive emissions of X-rays are generated, which can be detected on earth.

There are numerous suspicious-looking sites in the sky but all of them are too remote to be of any practical use to the would-be time-traveller. This predicament has prompted some scientists into considering alternative forms of time-tampering. Frank Tipler, a respected American scientist, has published several ideas for time machines in reputable journals such as the Physical Review and Annals of Physics. Tipler's design for a time machine involves a lot of abstruse mathematics and the dynamics of rotating cylinders. All of the work centres on twisting time and space with high-speed rotation devices but, as far as we know, no one has tried out Tipler's machines. However, the technology does exist to make some headway with Tipler's designs. NASA technicians are currently developing high-speed dynamo flywheels to power satellites and manned spacecraft. These flywheels are the size of a bicycle wheel and capable of 90,000 revolutions per minute. The outer rim of the wheel travels at more than 7,000mph, generating kilowatts of electricity to power up the space stations of the future. Some wheels now on the drawing board, will be magnetically-suspended on frictionless, superconducting axles. The speeds of these flywheels will be even more phenomenal and it will be interesting to see if they produce any time distortion, as predicted by Tipler.

Of course, we have only been concentrating on man-made time-travel. Could it be that time occasionally malfunctions all by itself through some poorly-understood phenomenon? Also, could the fabric of space-time down here on earth have weak spots or holes which could provide us with an opportunity to explore another era? With a magnification of 30 million, the electron microscope taught us that nothing in the universe has a smooth surface. The apparent smoothness of a pane of glass, or the veneered top of a coffee table is, in reality, pitted and pockmarked with grooves and chasms. Could the same be true of the space-time fabric? If the space-time continuum does have weak spots and holes in it, it could explain some of the following timewarp cases.

In the summer of 1992, a successful Cestrian entrepreneur and experienced pilot called Mr Davies, took off from a private airfield on the outskirts of Chester. He was at the controls of a Cessna and was headed for Liverpool's Speke Airport. As the Cessna was passing over the Stamford Bridge area, he noticed something quite strange. Thousands of feet below, there were no signs of the M53 or M56 motorways, nor indeed of a single A or B road. Intrigued and somewhat alarmed at the apparently missing roads, Mr Davies descended to take a closer look at the now unfamiliar territory. What he saw made his heart somersault – a tight formation of men was marching down a road towards a long rectangular squat building. He located a pair of 10 x 50 binoculars and trained them on the marching figures. They were Roman soldiers, and the building they were walking towards looked like some sort of Roman villa. At this point, a strange low mist materialised and enshrouded the landscape below. When it cleared, there was the A548 motorway and Mr Davies saw, to his relief, that everything had returned to normal. He flew over the M56 and decided to circle back to try and get a glimpse of the soldiers again but they were nowhere to be seen. Subsequently, he made extensive inquiries to ascertain whether the soldiers had been extras in a film. But there were no films about Romans being shot anywhere in Cheshire, or anywhere in Britain for that matter. He gradually realised that he had somehow ventured into the airspace of Cheshire during the Roman occupation of over a thousand years ago and has since learnt that several other pilots have experienced strange time-displacements in the skies over Cheshire. One highly-respected helicopter pilot, with a military background, lost radio communication during his episode but has never provided exact details of what took place. He did state that his greatest fear was of being stranded in the past. Perhaps this was the fate of Flying Officer Brian Holding.

On March 7th 1922, Holding took off from the airfield at Chester, on what was intended to be a short flight over the border to an airstrip in Wales. On the return journey from Wales, Holding's plane was spotted by scores of witnesses droning through the skies towards Chester. That plane and its experienced pilot never reached the airfield and were never seen again. A massive search for wreckage was launched but no trace of the craft was ever found. Stranger still, weeks before Holding flew into limbo, peculiar lights were seen flying in formation over North Wales.

Some timeslips have apparently given witnesses glimpses of the future. Between 1995 and 1997, a number of people in the vicinity of

Runcorn Bridge reported seeing a breathtaking futuristic vista on the horizon towards Hale Bank, near Speke Airport. The incredible sight that greeted the eyes of Frank Jones at 4am on the morning of December 5th 1995, was not the lights of Liverpool Airport – he thought it looked more like Liverpool Spaceport. The scene was like something from Close Encounters of the Third Kind. Enormous, lenticular ships, dotted with bright blue and red lights, were rising into the dark sky until they were out of sight. The domed ships were taking off silently from an enormous circular area which was lit with an actinic glow from powerful lights. Dotted about this launch area were towers and buildings speckled with a myriad of coloured lights.

As Mr Jones travelled north along Queensway, on the other side of the Mersey, he lost sight of the spectacle but knew dozens of other early morning commuters must have witnessed the UFOs. Several reports did trickle into the local radio stations and newspaper offices. That same week, a man crossing Runcorn Bridge said an enormous craft, shaped like an upturned basin, had hovered over his vehicle until he reached the Bridgewater Expressway.

The spectacular sightings abated for a while, then returned throughout 1996. Early in 1997, a woman from Halton Lodge, Warrington was terrorized by a gigantic spacecraft which loomed over her car as she crossed Runcorn Bridge. The terrified woman said the craft looked like the ominous Death Star from Star Wars. In a state of total panic, she deliberately sped across the bridge at 80mph in the hope that a policeman would see her speeding and come to her aid. Throughout the desperate getaway attempt, the colossal, overhead ship matched her speed and the woman thought she would be abducted but the circular spacecraft left her alone and continued on a slow trajectory towards Hale Bank, where Mr Jones had seen the mirage of a spaceport.

Several local ufologists quizzed the witnesses and descended on Hale Bank in search of any physical evidence left by the giant UFOs but found nothing. Were the ships UFOs from another planet, or did the witnesses see some future spaceport which will one day stand near Hale Bank and Speke Airport? Time will tell.

Without a doubt, one of the most intriguing timewarp incidents of recent years unfolded in the autumn of 1984 at Meadow Cottage, a small terraced house in the village of Dodleston near Chester. Ken Webster, a teacher, was working on his BBC personal computer late one night and inadvertantly left it on. When he returned to it some time later, he was surprised to see that a poem of some sort had been typed on the screen. At first, Webster suspected someone was pulling his leg but a hoax was soon ruled out when further messages came through. There was no modem connected to the computer, which only had 32K of memory. Even the floppy disk in the machine's drive was checked but there were no suspicious files hidden on it. Webster's home also became the focus of poltergeist activity. The cooker and heavy furniture were hurled about by an invisible force and cups and cans of food were stacked into parallel towers. Strange messages, signed 'Tomas', were also scratched on the floor and wall in an elegant calligraphy.

The eerie messages continued, most of them written in a quirky, mock-Tudor style. Webster tried to communicate with the mysterious writer via his computer and received several startling replies. There were six people communicating with him from somewhere, back in the 17th century. But how could people from the Elizabethan period contact a teacher in the 20th century by computer? That was never answered.

The main communicator identified himself as Tomas Harden and the following message, which occupied three screens of the computer, was analysed by experts in archaic language and even the staff of the Oxford English Dictionary, who could not detect a hoaxer at work. The message from Mr Harden runs:

'Myne goodly friend, I muste needs say, how cometh this, that there are manye thyngs for whiche I hath no rekenyng. Me thinketh it, that if thou cannot telle thee for what art in myne home, then I can namoor helpe yow than if myne witts had gone. I hath no kinfolk to fynd, myne wif was wreched with thy pestilence and the Lord didst take here soule and her unbore son (1517). Myne farme 'tis humble but it hath a pretty parcel o land, it hath redstoon footyngs and cleen rushes on myne beeten floor. This season I hath much to do, I hath to sow myne barly for myne ale, 'tis this that is myne craft and for whiche I am beste atte I fancy. Also I hath to go to Nantwhiche to myne cowthe freend Richard Wishal whois farme be so greet as to turn a four yeer rotacion o fallow. I do envye him he hath much there, but nought that delits me moor than

his cheese it cannot be equalled by any other for pleasantness of taste and wholesomness of digestion. I shall als calle atte Nantwyche Market 'tis not so greet as Cestre market by thy crios but 'tis of som desport. I shal need to go to Cestre this season to get myne soes, myne goodly freend Tomas Aldersay, a tailor by craft, makes them sometymes, I als mayketh soes but non of myne swyne are reedy 'tis far costly unlest I need kil one. Do you knoweth the country of Cestre the Water Gate is a plas that bringeth manye traders 'tis a shame the port doth shrynk I can record greet shipps now they grow small by each tyde, but Cestre port is still greeter than that o Leverpoole I am oft to the east wall of Cestre. Cow Lane, 'tis not so tyresome than that by the crois that it when myne fowl or swyne doth not trip up myne poore body I hear telle that thou art a teache in Hawardine doth yow meeneth Haodine cloth, thou stil earn thy greetly sum of twenty pounds per yeer I recorde myne unfavourable dean Henry Mann, who is likened to a fissh 'If any boy shal appear naturally avers to learning aft fair trial he shalt be expelled else wher lest lik a drone he should devour the bees honey'. Ney I cannot make merry on holy day for feer of myne lif myne freen was once a floytinge on a holy day did hath hus ears pinned to thy wood bloc methinks when thou sayeth Dodleston yow meeneth Dudlestun. Myne Queen is of cource Katherine Parr.'

The Society for Psychical Research (SPR) was invited to investigate and accepted the invitation. The SPR is a highly professional and unbiased investigative body of scholars and scientists which examine alleged paranormal incidents. The SPR was founded in 1882 and has investigated thousands of hauntings and mediums using strict scientific method. Many mediums were debunked by the SPR and a lot of hauntings were also discredited, but the SPR investigation into Ken Webster's seemingly haunted computer, resulted in an electrifying development. The SPR investigators left ten secret questions on the computer screen, out of sight of Mr Webster and, although the questions were not answered directly, messages came through on the screen referring to the questions, which naturally fazed the SPR people. This ruled out any deception and one of the investigators urged the sinister communicator to reply to the questions. A chilling reply came back. The communicator would only give an answer, if the investigator was willing to lose his soul. The SPR man backed off.

The BBC computer was later stripped and experts scrutinised its printed circuit boards, monitor, disk drive, keyboard, every inch of the machine, but there were no hidden radio transceivers and no modem. In those days, the Internet in Britain was just a programmer's pipe dream.

The SPR people were completely baffled and withdrew from the cottage without even making a report. Because the chief investigator made himself unavailable and never got back to Ken Webster, he became frustrated at the ham-fisted inquiry and wrote a book about his bizarre experience called The Vertical Plane.

In April 1986, Tomas Harden announced that he was going to leave the area and, after a few more messages, the 17th century computer hacker ceased communication.

The aformentioned timewarp cases seem to indicate that all time is eternally present, so to speak; that all of the historical periods of the past, present and future are contained within each other like Russian dolls. As you read this book right now, perhaps beyond the wafer-thin dimension of the present, a ravenous sabre-toothed tiger of the Pleistocene Era is prowling through your room. Until we learn how to manipulate time, we will go through this life as if our heads were facing back to front; we only know where we have been and where we are but can never know where we are going.

The mummified lady

The fear of being buried alive haunted the morbid imagination of the young Hannah Beswick of Birchen Bower House in Hollinwood. Although this spoilt child of a wealthy family was a chronic hypochondriac, her primary phobia was not unfounded, as she had heard of an unfortunate middle-aged man who had recently been buried alive at Hale. This was the middle of the 18th century and medical science was not sufficiently advanced to recognise the states of coma and cataplexy. Many unfortunate people fell into such states of immobility and their faint, whispering heartbeats and feeble pulses often went undetected. Some of these people actually regained consciousness while they were being slit open during the post-mortem and there are many hideous tales of anatomy students fainting at the sight of a revived specimen 'corpse', screaming in agony with its viscera pouring out of its abdomen.

The unfortunate premature burial at Hale was only discovered when the coffin was dug up because the 'dead' man's wife forgot to put her husband's bible in his casket. But when the coffin was opened, the gravediggers and the widow were confronted with a chilling scene that would have thrilled Edgar Allan Poe. The man's forehead was gashed and bruised because he had evidently regained consciousness and tried repeatedly to get up in the awful terminal darkness of his buried coffin. In a terrible fit of panic, the poor man had also clawed at the lid until his fingernails dripped with blood. He had finally died of oxygen starvation.

Young Hannah Beswick felt faint when she heard of this tragedy and she suffered recurring nightmares about being trapped in the stifling confined blackness, six feet underground, where her screams would be out of earshot.

A personal tragedy was to turn this fear into a life-long phobia. One of Hannah's brothers fell ill and was pronounced dead. The body was washed and dressed ready for burial. The undertakers recoiled as they laid it in the coffin, because it opened one eye and the body gave a corresponding twitch. The eyeball rolled and closed and the undertakers were about to dismiss the flickering eye and spasm as mere reflex nerve actions, often seen in a corpse, when the body opened both its eyes and tried to speak. This was no finicky nerve; the boy was still alive and, as if to prove it, let out a scream. The youth recovered and complained to the undertakers about the brutish, heavy-handed manner in which they had washed and dressed him.

Hannah was horrified by her brother's narrow escape and she almost suffered a breakdown. She developed a fear of falling asleep at night because she dreaded being unable to wake up and, through this irrational phobia, the stressed-out girl would often wake and find herself incapable of opening her eyes or moving a muscle; sometimes she couldn't even continue breathing because of the psychosomatic paralysis.

In 1757, old Hannah Beswick passed away and would have shared the fate that lies at the end of most of our lives but she cheated the grave for quite a while. You see, wealthy Lady Beswick had made bizarre stipulations in her will. The old woman had charged her physician, Dr Thomas White, with the task of mummifying her. To induce the doctor into carrying out this peculiar duty, Lady Beswick had named him as her chief beneficiary and, accordingly, left him the stupendous sum of £25,000. There were other strange conditions which Dr White was to carry out; he was to keep Lady Beswick's embalmed corpse above ground for over a hundred years and, once a year, he was to inspect the cadaver with two witnesses, to make sure she was dead. Lady Beswick's will also specified another requirement; every twenty-one years, her body was to be brought home to Birchen Bower and left there for a week.

Dr White gladly accepted the thousands of pounds and duly had his eccentric former patient embalmed 'by the best techniques of Paris and London'. In reality, Dr White preserved the old lady's corpse with tar, before swathing it in bandages, leaving only the face uncovered. The mummy was then surreally accommodated in the case of a glass-fronted grandfather clock. As if that wasn't bizarre enough, Dr White later put the grandfather clock on the roof of his Sale home! Each year afterwards, he would go up to his roof with two witnesses and pronounce the mummy dead, after a solemn inspection.

When the twenty-one years had elapsed, the mummy was taken home to Birchen Bower, where it was stored in the granary and, in the week the corpse was kept there, there were some supernatural occurrences. Pigs and sheep vanished, only to be found miles away. One of the cows was found in a confused state in a hayloft. Around this time, Birchen Bower had been converted into tenements and many tenants reported seeing the terrifying apparition of a radiant figure, with luminous blue eyes, which matched the description of Lady Beswick. One poor tenant, a hand-loom weaver named Joe, had a very close encounter with Lady Beswick's ghost which resulted in an unexpected financial reward. Joe was startled to see the luminescent phantom pointing to a large flagstone. When the ghost vanished, Joe lifted this flagstone and discovered a buried tin chest which contained a collection of small gold ingots. It is now known that this treasure was gold that Lady Beswick had hidden in 1745 when she feared that Bonnie Prince Charlie would come to Manchester and seize her wealth. Joe took the ingots to Manchester and sold them. He became a rich man overnight.

In keeping with the will's terms, Dr White eventually bequeathed the clockwork coffin's grisly contents to his former pupil and colleague, Dr Ollier, in 1776. When the latter passed away, the mummy of Hannah Beswick wound up at the Manchester Natural History Museum, where it was on view to those with a fascination for the macabre. The final home, above ground, of the itinerant corpse, was Owens College in Manchester but the trustees ultimately decided it was time to lay Hannah to rest in the tradition to which she had such an aversion. And so, on 22 July 1868, more than a hundred years after her death, Lady Beswick was given a proper Christian burial in Harpurhey Cemetery.

But that is not the end of this strange story. Not long after the burial, the solid-looking ghost of Lady Beswick was seen flitting about at Birchen Bower. A century afterwards, the restless phantom haunted the Ferranti factory which was later built on the land once occupied by Birchen Bower. The ghost also put in many appearances at nearby Cairo Mill in the early 1970s and terrorized several security guards during her phantasmagoric, after-dark stints. Some people say the mummy's ghost can still be seen prowling in the dead of night.

Chilling premonitions

Premonitions, by all logical and rational criteria, ought to be impossible, as the future has yet to take place. That's what reason tells us and yet there are, on record, many cases of people glimpsing future events – mentioned elsewhere in this book under the chapter entitled, Cheshire Timewarps. Here are just a few examples of 'coming events casting their shadows before' which have occurred within Cheshire.

In 1997, Richard and Suzy Hammond were shopping in the Bridge Street area of Chester. The couple had just bought some jewellery for their niece's birthday and decided to turn into the next thoroughfare, which was Eastgate Street. As the Hammonds were passing beneath the Eastgate Clock, one of the town's most famous landmarks, Suzy noticed three old women standing nearby. One was whimpering while another held her hand over her mouth and kept saying,

'Oh, my God.'

Suzy burned with curiosity and asked one of the women what was wrong and the answer that she received still haunts her,

'Di's dead.'

'Di? Princess Di?'

'Yes. She's died in a car crash with that Dodi fellah,' came the shocking reply from another of the women. Richard Hammond shook his head pensively then asked,

'When did it happen?'

There was a sinister change in the behaviour and mood of the three women. Their faces became expressionless simultaneously and they just strolled on in silence. Richard assumed they were deaf and hadn't heard his question and he and his wife set off to their home in Neston. As Richard drove his car into the drive, he wound down the window and asked his neighbour, Terry, if he'd heard about Princess Diana's fatal car crash. Terry shook his head and replied,

'No, why? Is she dead?'

'That's what we heard.'

He went into the house and turned on the TV. Suzy turned on the radio because it was almost 4pm but there was no mention of Diana or any crash on the news bulletin. Richard checked the teletext and dialled up the newsflash number but there wasn't even a mention of Di. Richard and Suzy were not royalists but they did think Diana was a kind and vulnerable woman who had been the victim of a cruel marriage.

Suzy concluded that the three women had obviously been winding them up but she still felt the whole incident was unusual and out of character for women in their mid-seventies. She felt there was something unearthly about the three pensioners and she later told her husband's friend, Roger, about the creepy incident.

That night, Roger and his girlfriend came over to the Hammond's home. They settled down with a few bottles of wine watching an old Alain Delon film, Borsalino, on BBC1. A newsflash caption interrupted the film and a sombre-looking newscaster announced that reports were coming in alleging that Princess Diana had been involved in a car crash in Paris and had suffered injuries as a result.

Suzy Hammond's heart skipped a beat and the conversation ceased. They all looked at each other in disbelief. The newsman allayed the viewers' fears slightly by adding that the reports suggested that Di's injuries were not thought to be lifethreatening. The newscaster said she had been in a car with Dodi Fayed and promised he would be back with more details as soon as they came in and the film continued.

Richard Hammond gulped down a glass of wine and shook his head. Then Suzy said,

'How did those old women know about this? They told us Di had been killed at two in the afternoon.'

'It could be just a bizarre coincidence. Di is still alive according to the reports.' No sooner had Roger finished his sentence, than the grave-looking newscaster reappeared to interrupt the film. In a broken voice, he broadcast the shocking news:

'We are getting reports in that Princess Diana has died...'

Suzy felt a glacial shiver down her spine and Roger uttered,

'Oh, God.'

On the following morning, Terry, the Hammonds' neighbour asked them how they had come to hear of Diana's death over nine hours before it had happened. When Suzy recounted her story about the three uncanny old women in Chester's Eastgate Street, Terry made an off-the-cuff comment that struck a chord and gave her the creeps.

'Maybe they were three witches.'

There is a weird epilogue to this incident. In December 1997, the Hammonds revisited Chester to do a spot of Christmas shopping and, there in Eastgate Street, at the exact same spot, stood the three old women who had made the disturbing prophecy. Suzy wanted to confront them to find out who, or what, they were but Richard sensed an immense aura of evil about the trio which made his flesh crawl and so he pulled his wife in the opposite direction, despite her protests. They have made three further visits to Chester but have always refrained from visiting that part of Eastgate Street where the clock is situated.

The second prophecy of this chapter also concerns a royal. Around the year 1612, a young pupil of King Edward's Grammar School in Macclesfield, had an awesome premonition which left him trembling. The boy was John Bradshaw and the bloodcurdling vision he had witnessed, while taking a short-cut through a cemetery, prompted him to scratch a seemingly nonsensical quatrain on the reverse of a gravestone:

My brother Harry must heir the land,
My brother Frank must be at his command,
While I, poor Jack, must do that,
Which all the world will wonder at.

People who came upon the odd rhyme wondered about its meaning and no one could make head nor tale of it. That is, until thirty-seven years had elapsed.

John Bradshaw went on to become a lawyer's clerk at Congleton when he left school and he developed such an ambition to become a barrister, that he decided to go to London to further his career by studying at Gray's Inn. In 1627, at the age of 25, he was called to the bar and held various appointments before returning to Congleton as a councillor-at-law to the corporation. In 1637 he was made both Mayor and Attorney General of Cheshire and Flintshire and, in 1644, he was engaged by Parliament to prosecute two Irish lords. He was absolutely ruthless and gained a widespread reputation thereafter as an immitigable, stony-hearted prosecutor. By 1646, he was promoted to become the Chief Justice of Chester.

Bradshaw held strong republican beliefs and, during the English Civil War, his sympathies were naturally with the Parliamentarian cause. In 1649, he was appointed President at the trial of the imprisoned King Charles I. It is recorded that on this solemn occasion, Bradshaw inflamed the court with a searing republican speech about the King's misgovernment and literally had his audience baying for the monarch's blood. The King, branded a tyrant, traitor and murderer, was convicted and John Bradshaw led the signing of the execution warrant. The King had refused to plead three times because he denied the court was a competent one and his refusals were treated as a confession. With the courage worthy of a martyr, King Charles I went to the scaffold in front of Whitehall on Tuesday 30 January 1649. The doomed Charles Stuart put on an extra shirt, in case the mob mistook his shivering for fear, on that bitterly cold day.

There was a delay in the execution proceedings because no one could be found to execute the King. The public hangman refused to do the job but two headsmen later turned up, disguised in masks and false beards and their identities have never been established. Minutes before he was beheaded, Charles told one executioner,

'I shall say but very short prayers,' and he gave the signal that he was ready to meet his barbaric fate by thrusting out his hands.

The crowd saw the axe flash down and the King was instantly decapitated. A huge groan erupted from the spectators. Then people from the mob paid to go up to the scaffold and the soldiers sold the curious ghouls pieces of wood which had been splashed with royal blood. The King's body was placed in a plain coffin and put in the Banqueting Hall, where the monarch's faithful friends held a candle-lit vigil. During the night, a sinister man in black, heavily muffled with a long cloak, visited the King's coffin. He was heard to mutter, 'Cruel necessity.' No one could be sure who the visitor was but many surmised it was either Cromwell or John Bradshaw.

Bradshaw often talked about the strange quatrain he had scrawled on the gravestone as a child and of the unsettling 'open-eye dream' which drove him to devise the rhyme. Bradshaw said that he had seen himself, almost 40 years in the future, signing the execution warrant of the King. This certainly made sense of the last two lines of the augural poem:

'While I, poor Jack, must do that, Which all the world will wonder at.'

In 1659, Bradshaw contracted the plague and died. Many thought that he had received this punishment for the crime of regicide. Upon the restoration of the monarchy in 1660, the corpses of Bradshaw, Cromwell and Ireton were dug up and ceremonially hanged at Tyburn.

Three centuries later, in September 1976 at Warrington, there was another case of a weird premonition which saved a girl's life. A 17-year-old bakery worker named Jenny, of Great Sankey, was walking to work with her mother at 5.30am. As they passed a construction site, Jenny heard an eerie female voice nearby repeatedly calling her name. She stopped in her tracks, straining her ears to locate the origin of the voice, which had a strange echo to it. It seemed to come from the direction of a wall next to the building site. Jenny's mother asked her what the matter was, as she couldn't hear the creepy woman's voice.

Jenny walked to the wall and peeped behind it but there was nobody there. This naturally spooked her and, from that moment on, she dreaded walking past the site on the way to work. Over the next fortnight, Jenny heard the same unearthly voice calling out her name almost every morning as she passed the building site. Jenny's mother felt it was all in her daughter's imagination as she hadn't been sleeping properly but the girl knew the ghostly voice wasn't hallucinatory. Her workmates were also sceptical and laughed at her claims.

Jenny successfully applied for a job as a cook with another company. Now she wouldn't have to walk past the haunted site any more. She celebrated by going out on the town with her workmates one night. But, when she returned from her night out, something very strange and terrifying took place. She hailed a taxi and got it to drop her off near to her home on a housing estate. She felt confident enough to take a convenient short cut down a dirt track, past the construction site. As she passed the wall, she was attacked by a tall, muscular man, who attempted to rape her. The attacker pulled the struggling teenager past the wall where she had heard the voice and forced himself on top of her. She screamed but the man slapped his large, rough hand down on her mouth, silencing her. Jenny tried to pull his hand off her mouth but the assailant reacted by gripping her throat and squeezing it hard. In sheer panic, Jenny's hand searched the ground beside her and, by some miracle, she felt a brick and grabbed it. Drawing on an inner anger, she smashed the brick into the man's head and he collapsed on top of her, crying with pain. Jenny pushed the brawny would-be rapist off her and screamed. A few neighbours came running to the teenager's aid, as the attacker stumbled off into the night, clutching his injured head.

Jenny was so traumatised by the attack, that she was unable to talk for months. With hindsight, she had the strange feeling that the voice she had previously heard was some sort of warning from the 'other side' or, perhaps, some guardian angel. She also felt it was strange how the brick had found its way into her hand. But for that brick, she would have been raped and possibly murdered.

Life-saving ghosts

From my extensive files on hauntings, the majority of ghosts are not malevolent at all. In fact, some of them can happily co-exist in a house full of living people with a minimum of interference. Even the disruptive poltergeist can occasionally settle down to a comical feeble presence amounting to a vanished set of keys, a tilted picture or, perhaps, an inexplicable change of TV channel. Some ghosts have even swung into action to help the living and there are many cases on record of spirits allegedly saving lives. Here are several such tales.

In the winter of 1933, Nora Redding, a 70-year-old spinster from Runcorn, was listening to her radio when she became aware of a strange rapping on the oven. The noise naturally startled the woman but when she went over to the cooker, she noticed that she had left one of the gas knobs turned on. Nora had no sense of smell and would not have known about the leaking gas if it had not been for the mysterious tapping. She opened the oven door and peered in. Finding it empty, she closed the door, opened the windows to let out the build up of gas and pondered on the nature of her mysterious helper. She wondered if it was a guardian angel at work but dismissed that line of reasoning as ludicrous. All the same, the phantom helper saved her from death and serious injury on several other occasions.

Once, when Nora was visiting her nephew in Liverpool, she went to step off the kerb to cross a busy Lime Street when she felt an invisible hand pull her backwards. A split second later, a goods wagon came careering round the corner. She later told her horrified nephew that it had been such a close shave, that the wagon had almost taken the buttons off her coat.

The most chilling salvation took place several years later one dark autumnal evening as the old woman listened to her favourite records on an old phonograph. The time was 8.15pm and she decided it was getting a trifle late to be playing her 78s, so she went to turn off the antique record player but was distracted from doing so by a rapping at the front door.

'Who is it?' She wasn't expecting any visitors and wondered, nervously, if she should put the bolts on the door.

'It's me,' came a low, masculine voice through the slightly-opened letter box.

'I said who is it?' Nora again demanded as she began to tremble.

'Is Mr Johnson there?' asked the stranger, as he peeped at Nora through the letterbox. His eyes were very dark and his eyebrows joined in the middle.

'There's no one of that name here.'

'I can't hear you, love. Could you open the door? Don't worry, I only live down the street by Mr Smith.'

'Wait a minute then.'

Nora had decided that the man was telling the truth and was reaching for the doorknob when, suddenly, the old phonograph started up of its own accord and the song 'Deep Purple', by Peter de Rose, began to play backwards. The unintelligible cacophony blared out, giving Nora and the shady caller a start. Then something strange occurred, which she was unable to explain to her dying day. The stylus of the malfunctioning phonograph became stuck in a groove and kept repeating a reversed excerpt from the song which sounded like a repetition of the word 'murderer'.

Nora believed it was a warning from the helpful spirit not to open the door and she let out a scream which sent the sinister caller running off into the darkness. Moments later, the phonograph came to a halt.

On the following day, she perused the local paper and saw, to her horror, that the police were hunting a violent confidence trickster who had attempted to rob an elderly woman at knifepoint, in the Runcorn area. When she told her nephew about the strange incident, he convinced his aunt to stay with him in Liverpool and the phantom protector never intervened in the spinster's life again.

In 1991 in Knutsford, a spectral heroine allegedly saved an infant from death. The Donaldsons were fast asleep one night, when their thirteen-month-old baby started to cry in his cot. Mrs Donaldson sat up, bleary-eyed and switched on the bedside lamp ready to go to her son, Aaron. What she saw, sent a shiver up her spine. A young girl, of around 17 or 18, with long black hair, was leaning over the cot, looking at the baby with a friendly, lopsided grin. She wore a long, old fashioned nightgown and her presence shocked Mrs Donaldson, who could only manage to cry out,

'Oi!'

Upon which, the girl vanished.

Mrs Donaldson shook her husband awake and told him about the ghostly apparition but he claimed she was dreaming. His wife insisted that she wasn't and had a hard time getting back to sleep. On several occasions during the night she thought she heard someone creeping about near the bed.

A fortnight later, something spooky happened, which made Mr Donaldson revise his sceptical dismissal of his wife's story. The time was 3.30am and Mrs Donaldson's scream startled her husband from his slumbers.

'What in God's name?' Mr Donaldson sat bolt upright and found his wife staring at something on the duvet. It was little Aaron, making a terrible choking sound. She picked her baby up and he vomited and, after crying and wheezing for a moment, started to breathe normally. The mystery was, how had the baby travelled the twelve feet from his cot in the corner of the room, onto his parent's bed. There was only one explanation; the ghostly girl had transported the child, as Mrs Donaldson claimed she had been wakened by someone tapping on her shoulder. It had not been her husband because he was facing away from her. A month later, Mr Donaldson was returning from the toilet, when he also saw the life-saving apparition standing by the cot, musing over his little sleeping son. He was frightened, even though the girl looked quite amiable and good-natured. As he turned on the light, she disappeared.

The ghost's identity remains a mystery but the couple regard her as a harmless character and would dearly like to thank her for saving their son's life. As Aaron grew older, the teenaged spectre's appearances sadly became more and more infrequent and she has not been seen for quite a while now. Perhaps if the couple have another child, the ghost who saved Aaron's life will return.

Phone calls from the dead

The familiar telephone seems the least likely object you'd associate with the supernatural but, over the years, there have literally been hundreds of reports of ghosts ringing people up.

In 1969, Karl Uphoff, a New Jersey rock musician, received a phone call from his grandmother. Nothing unusual about that you might think but his gran had passed away two days earlier. Karl was eighteen at the time of the phantom call and there had always been a special bond between himself and his deaf grandmother. She used to phone up his friends and ask,

'Is Karl there?' but, because she knew she wouldn't be able to hear the reply, she would then say,

'Tell him to come home at once.'

Karl's friends were irritated by the old woman's constant calling and complained about him having given out their numbers. Eventually, Karl's gran died and he was naturally upset but had no leanings towards spiritualism and consequently never expected to hear from her again.

One evening in 1969, Karl was with his friends in the basement of an apartment in Montclair, New Jersey, when his friend's mother came down and announced that Karl was wanted on the phone. As he listened to the caller, he realised that it was his recently-deceased gran. Before he could ask her how she could possibly talk to him when she was dead, she hung up. Many more calls followed but, on each occasion, when she was asked how she was still able to communicate, or what the 'other side' was like, she would hang up. Finally, the calls stopped but Karl felt strongly that she was still watching over him.

Another chilling phone call from beyond the grave allegedly occurred in Wilmslow, Cheshire in 1977, when a young woman, Mary Meredith, received a call from her cousin, Shirley, in Manchester. Mary shuddered when she heard Shirley's voice on the crackly line because, only minutes before, Mary had received a telephone call from her auntie, telling her of Shirley's tragic death in a car crash, just an hour ago. Again, before the phantom caller could be questioned, she hung up.

In 1995, a radio station in Liverpool featured a medium named James Byrne in a weekly show. Mr Byrne was a psychic who claimed he could convey messages from the next world and was a very popular guest. In fact, he was so popular, callers would jam the switchboard whenever he was on air. A Mrs Wilson, of Ellesmere Port, rang the radio station, desperate to get in touch with James Byrne because her grandfather had died a year ago and she wanted to know if he had any messages for her. Unfortunately, she couldn't get through to the medium as the lines were jammed solid, so she just sat back and listened to him on the show.

Around 10 o'clock, just as News at Ten was starting, Mrs Wilson's phone rang. The woman answered the call and a familiar but distant-sounding voice said,

'Look love, I'm alright. It's great over here; I'm with your gran and all the other nice people who have passed on.'

Mrs Wilson was naturally astounded, for she recognised the caller as her late grandfather and she managed to mutter,

'Grandad! Is that you?'

'Yeah, love. Now listen. Stop living in the past and reminiscing. Go forward. I'm still around looking over you. I've got to go now, love. Give my love to the kids. Bye.'

As Mrs Wilson listened to the purring tone, she wondered if someone was perpetrating a sick joke, so she dialled 1471, in order to get the caller's number but the automated voice on the line quoted her own number. In other words, the call had originated from her own telephone. She had no extension and was therefore convinced that her grandfather had somehow called her from beyond the grave, to reassure her.

In the late 1980s, Sadie, a Mancunian woman, lost her husband in tragic circumstances. She was left a considerable amount of money in his will and she and her 7-year-old daughter, Abigail, subsequently moved to a graceful old cottage, just outside Sandbach. The landlord only asked for a modest sum as a deposit and Sadie wondered why the rent was so low for such a desirable rustic residence. She and Abigail gave the dusty, cobwebbed place a good spring-cleaning and later had it decorated. She fell in love with the peaceful rear garden, which had a mournful-looking weeping willow in the middle of its neglected lawn. One December evening, three months after moving in, Abigail excitedly told her mother that she had just seen a kindly old woman, in a long black dress, smiling at her beneath the willow tree. She claimed that the woman had waved once, then faded away.

Abigail was a quiet, honest child, who was not in the habit of imagining things and embroidering fanciful stories, so Sadie was a little unnerved by her daughter's tale of the ghostly woman. However, there were no further sightings of the phantom, although many strange things did occur at the cottage shortly afterwards.

One night, Abigail said she felt dizzy. Sadie put her daughter to bed earlier than normal, convinced she was just overtired, having risen earlier than normal that day and having helped out in the garden, digging up weeds. She decided she would have an early night herself and retired to her bedroom with a book. An hour had passed when there was a knock at the front door. Sadie was naturally alarmed and wondered who could be calling at 11pm. She went downstairs to the hall in her slippers and nightgown and nervously asked who was there.

A well-spoken man replied that he was a doctor and that he had been called out to examine a girl named Abigail. She unbolted the door and opened it. A tall, grey-haired man stood on the doorstep, carrying a briefcase. He consulted a card in his hand and asked,

'You are Sadie?' Apparently, he also knew her surname.

Sadie explained that she had not called him out but invited the physician indoors anyway. She escorted him up to Abigail's bedroom and he gave the child a quick examination. He pointed out a rash on her arms and, after shining his torch into her eyes, told Sadie that it looked as if she had the symptoms of meningitis. The doctor drove the girl and her shocked mother to hospital, where she was positively diagnosed but, because it was caught in its early stages, the antibiotics and other treatment fortunately overcame the life-threatening disease.

But who had called the doctor out? Sadie didn't have any idea at the time but something happened later which gave her a good idea of the eerie helper's identity.

In 1989, a handsome man called at the cottage. He claimed his car had run out of petrol and asked the widow if she could possibly lend him a few pounds to fill his can at the station down the road. He offered to leave an expensive-looking watch as security and promised he would return later to repay her. She kindly gave the sincere-looking man a five-pound note and he appeared very grateful. He walked off to the filling station with his can, then returned to his Ford Fiesta, which was parked in the lane. After putting the petrol in the tank, he returned to give the widow the change from the fiver she had lent him. He promised to set off immediately to get the rest of the money he owed her and, although Sadie insisted it wouldn't be necessary, he left. He returned at about six that evening with the money and a bunch of carnations. She was flattered and, as she accepted the flowers, he kissed her hand then turned, ready to walk away. She suddenly said to him,

'Wait; you forgot your wristwatch.'

'Oh yes, thanks, I nearly forgot,' and he retraced his steps up the path.

'Come in and have a cuppa.'

It had been quite some time since Sadie had enjoyed any male company and she found the man attractive. Over a cup of tea, she discovered that he was from Middlewich and that his name was Tim. In the course of a long conversation, which lasted until 9 'o' clock, she also learned that his steady girlfriend of four years had recently left him for someone else, leaving him wary of getting involved with the opposite sex again. She advised him not to become a recluse because of his experiences with one girl and hinted that she was still looking for someone too. She was almost forty but looked about thirty-five and he was twenty-six. She considered that the age gap between them wasn't too great and the evening ended with an exchange of telephone numbers.

Two days later, Sadie telephoned Tim but got a steady, disconnected tone. She wondered if the young man had given her a dead number, just to appease her. She didn't know what to think but she hoped he would contact her again. A few days later, the cottage phone started to ring. Abigail picked it up as Sadie was racing towards it.

'It's for you, Mum.'

Sadie grabbed the receiver,

'Hello?'

But the voice on the end of the line wasn't Tim's. It was the voice of an old woman, who proceeded to recount some horrible details about Tim from Middlewich. She claimed he was a bigamist and a confidence trickster, who knew about Sadie's large inheritance. She was stunned by the claims and a little heart-broken. She asked the caller to identify herself and was told to ask the landlord.

Tim paid another visit to the cottage on the Sunday evening of the following week, bringing more flowers and a bottle of wine. Sadie confronted him with the anonymous caller's allegations. As soon as he caught the gist of what she was saying, he leapt up, put on his coat and left the cottage without saying a word. The widow never set eyes on him again and, several months later, she learned from a neighbour that he was regarded as a thoroughly shady character, who had spent six months in prison for fraud. He was also rumoured to have two wives; one in Crewe and another in Chester but was currently living with a mistress in Middlewich.

When Sadie's landlord visited her shortly afterwards, she told him about the mysterious old woman's strange warning. The landlord seemed very nervous all of a sudden, especially when she told him that the uncanny caller had claimed that the landlord knew her identity.

Ultimately, the landlord admitted that the cottage's previous occupants had reported seeing the ghost of an old woman. They had also complained of creepy, late-night nuisance calls from an old woman who gave advice and warnings. He claimed that he had initially dismissed the stories as exaggerations and an excuse to leave without paying the rent. Sadie, however, promised that she would not move out because she regarded the ghost as helpful and harmless, upon which the landlord then told Sadie that an old spinster named Enid had died at the cottage five years back. She had lived there for some twenty years and was something of a recluse. There were rumours that she had been jilted in her youth and had never bothered with men again. The only thing she lived for was the back garden. One afternoon she was found dead beneath the willow tree that she had so lovingly tended. The coroner ruled that Enid had died from a massive stroke but, within months, the new tenants reported seeing her spectre crossing the lawn, one moonlit night. The landlord confessed that he had also glimpsed Enid's shade one wintry evening. He saw her glide across the snow-covered lawn but, when he went to investigate, there were no footprints in the virgin snow.

The ghost hasn't phoned for a while but, whenever the phone rings, Sadie often wonders if it is Enid calling. She still hasn't found Mr Right and, although Abigail is now married, her mother doesn't feel lonely, because she knows Enid is always around somewhere.

Are you expecting any phonecalls tonight?...

The busman's curse

Throughout the ages, in all nations, curses have been feared. A curse is an invocation of malevolence, a psychological weapon from the routine armoury of the magician, shaman, or ill-wisher. Today, the psychologists would be quick to dismiss a curse as a simple form of suggestion and explain that a 'hex' would only be capable of harming a person who is superstitious, gullible or expecting trouble in the first place. That would seem to be the rational explanation; the only trouble is that this interpretation fails to account for the many cases that have taken effect on a victim, despite his disbelief in the mumbo-jumbo world of the supernatural. Take the case of Robert Heinl, a retired US Marine Corps colonel, who had served on Haiti for six years as the chief of a naval mission.

Shortly after his retirement, Heinl wrote a book about the history of Haiti, which criticised the ruling dynasty of Francois 'Papa Doc' Duvalier. He was later amused to learn from the newspapers that a curse had been placed on his book. Heinl dismissed the curse as a poor example of psychological warfare – then a streak of misfortune fell upon him. The manuscript of his book went missing; the ex-colonel fell through a stage while giving a speech, badly injuring his leg; a Washington Post journalist who was about to interview him about his book was struck down with acute appendicitis; a large stray dog attacked him near his home, inflicting a serious bite and finally, on 5th May 1979, Heinl was on holiday with his wife on St Barthelemy Island, near Haiti, when he suddenly dropped dead from a heart attack. His widow later remarked,

'There is a belief that the closer you get to Haiti, the more powerful the magic becomes.'

In the mid-1980s, a similar fatal curse was made; not by a Voodoo magician, but by a middle-aged Cheshire busman from Poynton, named Frank.

In 1986, Frank scrimped and saved to buy a brand new, front-loading video recorder and colour television for his autistic, 12-year-old nephew, Richie. Richie was overjoyed with the gift and Frank bought the boy a couple of Disney videos.

One evening at 9pm, Frank returned to his flat and saw that the front door was partly open. At first, he thought that his nephew had left it open, as Frank had given him a key to the flat, so he could use the video. He had intended that Richie keep the video in his own home but he loved Frank's company and preferred coming to his flat.

As Frank entered the living room, his heart missed a beat. The video had gone but the new colour television was still there. There was one curious clue; the glass covering a framed photograph of Richie had been cracked. The photo had rested on the video, so it seemed that the thief had knocked it down during the robbery but, for some reason, had taken the trouble to put the photo back in its place. Frank wondered if his nephew was the culprit but the child burst into tears when he learned that his cherished video had been stolen.

Frank went to the pub to drown his sorrows and told his best mate, Derek, about the robbery. Derek patted him on the back, bought him a pint of bitter and promised to keep his eyes open for a second-hand video to replace the stolen one. Suddenly, Frank's anger got the better of him,

'I can't understand how anyone could do such a thing. I hope something terrible happens to the coward who took that video!'

The landlady and most of the drinkers in the pub, were shocked by this sudden outburst but Frank continued to rant on about the robbery. After attempting to calm him down, Derek went off to the toilet.

'I put a curse of death on the person who robbed Richie's video! I hope he drops down dead! I do!'

Seconds later, another friend of Frank's, named Andy, came into the pub and ordered a pint. He noticed that Frank looked irritated and red-faced, and asked him what was the matter. Andy's reaction to the sad tale took Frank by surprise. Instead of showing sympathy, he just gave a sidelong smirk and scoffed,

'Come off it, Frank. You must think I was born yesterday.'

'What're you on about?'

'Everyone knows it was an insurance job.' Andy smirked, calmly sipping his pint of mild.

'What?' Frank spluttered. He wanted to give Andy a thump for the outrageous claim. Andy smiled and leaned forward to whisper to Frank,

'I saw Derek coming out of your place with the video this evening at eight.'

'You're kidding.' Frank said with a shocked expression. Now it all made sense. Derek had put the cracked picture of Richie on the TV. Then Frank realised something else. Two weeks ago, the spare Yale key to his flat had gone missing. Derek must have taken it during one of his visits. Andy had presumed that Frank had arranged for his best mate to fake the robbery, so he could get the insurance money and sell the video.

Frank was furious and he stormed off to the toilets to have words with his so-called friend but, when he went into the gents, he found Derek lying dead on the floor.

A post-mortem recorded the cause of Derek's death as natural causes, but Frank was convinced that the curse he had put on the robber of the video, had taken Derek's life.

That is not the end of the story. In 1992, Frank's car was stolen as he was visiting his cousin in Prestbury. When he came out of his cousin's house, he glimpsed a red-haired man driving off in his car. When police found the vehicle, the thief had removed the radio-cassette player. The thief had also taken an envelope from the glove compartment, containing a set of photos of Frank's mother, who had died just a few weeks back. Even worse, the thief had ripped up and scattered the prized photographs. The keys to the car were also missing. Frank was more upset about the torn-up photographs, than the state of his car.

Two days later, Frank was driving his bus through Bramhall, when an old friend boarded the vehicle and said he had heard about Frank's car being stolen. Without thinking, Frank said,

'I hope that, whoever ripped up those photographs of my Mum, meets a terrible death.'

He uttered these words at precisely 4.30 in the afternoon. At that exact time, there was a car crash on the single carriageway, practically in front of Frank's bus. The driver was catapulted through the windscreen, as the vehicle smashed into a concrete lampost. He bounced along the pavement and Frank stopped the bus and ran with his friend to the man's aid. The casualty on the pavement was the red-haired man who had robbed Frank's car a couple of days previously and torn up the pictures. He was dead from his injuries. The police later confirmed him as the robber and he still had Frank's car keys on him. At his home, they found twelve radios ripped from various cars, including Frank's.

Once again, Frank had the eerie impression that he had put a fatal curse on another person who had wronged him.

Were the two deaths just coincidence, or the result of the ancient and well-documented powers of the death curse?

Dead beat

The following creepy incident took place in Crewe in the 1950s.

In 1955, Robert Page, a filling station attendant in Crewe, was preparing to finish work around 10pm, when his colleague, Teddy Gleddel, phoned to tell him that his wife had just gone into labour with their second child and couldn't make his shift.

When Robert phoned his wife, Kate, to tell her he would be home later, she was at her mother's. At around 1am, she returned to their flat, put the milk bottles out and hung up her coat. She was so tired, she walked up to the bedroom and, without turning on the light, undressed by the light of a streetlamp. She kicked off her shoes, undid her blouse and slipped off her dress and underwear. She glanced at the bed and assumed her husband was sleeping there, then got under the covers.

She kissed Robert, but he didn't react. She tried to arouse some passion in him by kissing his ear and gently stroking his hair but Robert was out cold. Kate turned over in a huff and muttered,

'I'm wasting my time as usual. What's happened to our love life? You're always too tired.'

Kate started to sniffle and a tear rolled from her eye. She began to question whether Robert still loved her. Perhaps he'd just been using her, or he'd met someone else. There was only one way to find out and that was to wake him up and confront him.

'Robert, Robert, wake up!' she shouted, shaking her husband repeatedly but with no effect.

Then she heard the sound of a key rattling in the front door. The sound terrified Kate. There had been a number of break-ins in the neighbourhood recently.

'Robert! Wake up! Someone's trying to break in.' She pinched her husband's arm and shook him.

The front door closed and heavy footsteps thudded up the stairs. The intruder was coming towards the bedroom. Kate was now paralysed with fear. Peeping over the blankets, she watched in horror as the handle of the bedroom door started to turn. The door opened and she let out a scream as she grabbed hold of Robert. The intruder switched on the bedroom light, revealing that he was not an intruder after all, but Robert Page, her husband. When Kate saw him standing there, she felt confused, then frightened. Who was the man in the bed with her? Her husband was certainly keen to know the answer too. Robert pulled the blankets back to reveal his naked wife snuggled up against a dead stranger.

'What the devil's going on?' he demanded and waited for an explanation from his wife. No wonder she hadn't asnwered his phone call.

Kate let out another scream when she saw the corpse lying next to her and leapt from the bed into the arms of her enraged husband. She explained everything and, although he was initially sceptical, he eventually accepted that she was telling the truth.

The presence of the body, which was that of a middle-aged man, was never explained. He had evidently died from natural causes but was never identified. Police surmised that he had perhaps been one of two burglars who had suffered a heart attack while breaking into the bedroom. It was speculated that the other burglar had panicked and tucked the body up in the bed, before fleeing. Another theory was that the man was a sex attacker, who had broken into Kate's bedroom and had lain in wait for her, before suffering a heart attack. The case was never solved, and is still an unfathomable mystery.

Halloween hauntings

On the night of the 31st October, which was the last day of summer in the old Celtic calendar, a festival was held to honour the Lord of the Dead, Samhain. Bonfires were lit to summon forth the spirits of the deceased to walk the earth again and the pagan peoples of those times had an unquestioning belief in the reality of the returning souls. The belief was so powerful, that even the introduction of Christianity could not eradicate the festival of Samhain and so the Church ended up hijacking the ancient feast. In AD 834, the Church elders decreed that All Saints Day was to be moved from 13th May to 1st November and henceforth, 31st October was to be known as, All Hallow's Eve (hallows was an ancient word for saints). In AD 988, the pagans of Britain were still honouring Samhain and the Church urged them not to pray to the dead but for them, via the saints. The Church's directive had little effect on the psyche of the largely superstitious population, who continued to believe that the departed souls would rise from their graves on Halloween and revisit their old homes to warm themselves at the fireside. Bonfires continued to be lit on Hallow's Eve and the Church elders desperately racked their brains trying to think of a Christian holy day that could be the focus for the archaic pyromania. Perhaps the bonfire day could be moved to some date when a Christian martyr was burnt at the stake. Ironically, the Halloween bonfire cult was later moved to Guy Fawkes Night, to mark the arrest of the conspirator on 5th November 1605.

However, the Church's attempts to sabotage and subvert the ancient Celtic festival were ultimately a dismal failure. Today nobody regards Halloween as the night before we pray to the saints; 31st October is synonymous with apple-bobbing (the vestige of a Roman custom), trick or treat, ghosts, witches flitting past the moon on broomsticks, goblins, vampires, skeletons, bogeymen, the devil, black cats, graveyards, candlelit pumpkin lanterns and so on. Halloween is an enduring tradition that refuses to die and here are three stories of the paranormal which allegedly took place on what is asserted to be the most ghostly night of the year...

On the night of Sunday 31st October 1976, Tony Baron, a bored security guard, was patrolling a warehouse in Warrington. At 10.45, he decided to light a cigarette and go up to the roof with his thermos flask of coffee.

The guard looked up at the full moon looming on the eastern horizon and inhaled some fresh air. He casually scanned the skyline of the town then looked down at the streets. He noticed the silhouettes of two girls chasing one another around the moonlit playground of a school about a hundred yards down the road. The girls had long hair and both looked roughly the same age, about sixteen or eighteen. Tony assumed they were sixth-formers, messing about in the deserted playground. Then they simply vanished as he watched.

Tony was so shocked by the sight of this vanishing double act, that his jaw dropped and his cigarette fell into his coffee. He continued staring at the playground to see if the figures would reappear but they didn't. He felt uneasy and went back inside the factory via a door in the roof. He had never believed in ghosts but knew that he had just seen the ghosts of two schoolgirls; it had not been a trick of the light or some hallucination. He telephoned his old uncle, Stan Jones, a retired policeman, to tell him about the strange spectacle. After he'd listened to Tony's strange account, Stan asked his nephew,

'Haven't you read the news recently?'

Tony confessed that he only read the sports pages of the newspapers.

'Why? What's that got to do with what I saw?'

'It was in the papers about a week back, two sisters died in a car crash up in Bolton. They were only fifteen and they both attended the school you're talking about.'

'You're kidding,' said Tony, feeling a cold chill pass over him.

Tony's uncle then made matters worse by relating a strange experience he'd had himself eleven years before – in the very warehouse Tony was guarding.

'It was around 1965 and, funnily enough, I recall it was also in October. In those days, the old nightwatchman used to let me in and I'd have a cuppa with him and a good natter. Anyway, on this October night, I turned up and the watchman poured me a cuppa and kindly offered me one of his sandwiches, then went to the toilet at the other end of the building. Now, I was never one for believing in ghosts and the supernatural and all that mumbo jumbo but, while the nightwatchman was gone, something happened which played on my mind for years. Perhaps I shouldn't tell you. It could play on your mind too.'

Tony didn't know whether he wanted to hear the rest of his uncle's tale. If he didn't, he knew he'd be wondering what he had seen all night.

'Go on, I'm not scared, Uncle Stan.'

'Well, just after the nightwatchman went to the loo, a horrible, penetrating chill filled the place. I could see my breath, it was that cold all of a sudden. Then, I got this really creepy feeling that there was some presence beside me.'

'How do you mean?' Tony asked, nervously fiddling with the coiled phone flex.

Stan paused, then said,

'It's hard to explain; it's like when people say they know when they're being watched. They can feel someone's eyes on them. It was like that. It became really tense in that place while the watchman was gone. And then I saw something. Sure you're not nervous?'

'Nah, I'm more curious than scared,' Tony lied, putting on a brave front.

'I saw these covered bodies lying in a row in a dark corner of the room. Three or four I think there were, covered in white sheets. I was really baffled. When the watchman came back, I asked him what they were but when I pointed to them, they had gone.'

'What did the watchman say? Did he see them?'

'The watchman didn't see the bodies but he knew what I was talking about, because he said he'd seen them a few times over the years.'

'That's really weird.' Tony said and he was now sensing, or perhaps imagining, a presence.

'You know what the watchman told me?' Stan asked his trembling nephew.

'No, what?'

'I thought he was having me on but your Auntie Hilda later confirmed it. He claimed that a morgue used to stand on the site of the warehouse.' Suddenly, the phoneline went dead.

Tony Baron felt the hairs on the nape of his neck standing up. He had the overwhelming feeling that something or someone was approaching from behind. It was then he noticed the foul smell pervading the place. What's more, something icy touched the back of his head. The guard ran off as fast as his legs could carry him and, with his heart pounding, he unlocked the main door of the warehouse. He ran out into the street and didn't stop running until he had a stitch in his side. He decided enough was enough and intended to hand in his notice at the warehouse in the morning. As his uncle's house was nearer than home, Tony paid him a late visit and told him about the spooky atmosphere which had just been too much for him to take. Then Stan said something which sent another shiver down his nephew's spine,

'As I was talking to you on the phone, the line went dead, so I waited. I thought something had happened to you. About thirty seconds later, a woman's voice said, "Tony's just run out of here," and she sounded as if she was mentally deranged because she started to laugh hysterically, then she banged the phone down. Who was she?'

'There was no one else on the premises,' Tony stammered in disbelief.

A year later, Tony was in a pub and he got talking to a middle-aged man who said he'd done a stint as a security guard in the same warehouse. He startled Tony by telling him that he had packed in his job because one night he had a cat nap and, when he woke up, a sinister-looking woman, in a long white gown, was standing over him, smiling. Her face was as white as a sheet and her eyes were yellowish with dark rings around them. There was also a disgusting smell, like the aroma of decomposing flesh, in the atmosphere. Seconds later, the woman cackled and vanished and the obnoxious odour quickly faded.

The identity of the phantom is a mystery but it is said that she still walks the warehouse in the dead of night. Perhaps she has some earthly tie with the old morgue that once stood on the site of the warehouse in the 19th century…

On Wednesday 31st October 1979, at 11.15pm, three girls in Northwich got more than they bargained for when they intended to get a glimpse of their future husbands by dabbling in the occult. The girls, all aged sixteen, were Emma, Melissa and Erika and they were minding the house for Emma's Auntie June, who was in hospital for a few days, recovering from an operation. The house was Victorian and quite a creepy place at night but the girls didn't notice the spooky atmosphere of the place initially. They were all too busy talking about the boys they fancied and Melissa, the bookish one, had an idea. She suggested carrying out an old Halloween custom which supposedly enabled you to see a vision of the person you would end up marrying.

Emma and Erika were quite excited at this magical prospect and asked Melissa how it was done. In a matter-of-fact manner she told them:

'You light two candles and place them on each side of you, then you look into a mirror, combing your hair with one hand and eating an apple at the same time. After a while, you see your future husband looking over your left shoulder in the mirror. My mum did it when she was a girl and saw my dad's face.'

'Let's do it!' Emma exclaimed, enthusiastically.

'It's got to be at midnight exactly.' Melissa told her excited friend. The time was only 10 o'clock in the evening.

Emma went out of the living room for a while, then returned with two scented candles, each mounted on a twisted silver candlestick. She also had a hairbrush taken from her aunt's bedroom. She positioned the candlesticks on opposite ends of the long mantlepiece, over the flickering coal fire, then gazed into the eyes of her reflection in the mirror situated over the fireplace. In a melodramatic voice, she joked,

'Who will you marry Emma?' and started to laugh.

'Don't mess about with the Black Arts; it's dangerous,' Melissa warned her flippant friend.

At precisely midnight, the heavy curtains were drawn and the traditional Halloween custom commenced. In the dark room, lit only by two candles and the flickering flames in the grate, Emma solemnly stared at her reflection in the mirror. Behind her, to her left, stood Melissa and Erika, holding on to each other's hands with electric excitement. They giggled at the sound of Emma crunching into the apple, then watched the dim sparks of static electricity crackle through the girl's hair as she pulled the brush through it.

'Keep staring at the space over the left shoulder of your reflection. Concentrate on that space as you brush.' Melissa coached Emma, who was taking it all very seriously.

Her friends waited behind her with bated breath, both yearning for something to happen.

And something did happen. Something which almost caused Emma to faint with shock.

A face emerged out of the darkness of the mirror and peered over the left shoulder of Emma's mirror image. It was a sinister, contorted, pallid face with reddish hair, snarling at her. Emma's natural reaction was to turn right, for she expected the terrifying, disembodied face to be hovering over her right shoulder but it wasn't there. It only existed in the mirror, as a reflection.

A sudden whistling draught from nowhere blew out the candles on the mantlepiece. Erika shrieked and dashed off to turn on the light but couldn't locate the switch and, in her panic, toppled over a chair.

By now, Melissa was rushing for the door and she tripped over Erika, who was sprawled across the floor. Emma suddenly yelled out in pain. A lump of orange-hot, incandescent coal had jumped out of the fireplace on its own and bounced off her arm. More and more fragments of glowing coal flew out of the fire and showered the room, until Emma raced to the lightswitch and managed to flick it on. Scattered about the room were smouldering lumps of coal, sizzling on the carpet and furniture. As Melissa and Erika fled from the living room into the hall, Emma bravely grabbed a pair of tongs from a stand on the hearth and used them to pick up the dangerous chunks of coal. She threw them back into the grate and, as soon as she saw that nothing was on fire, she hurried out of the house and stayed at Erika's place for the remainder of that night.

The girls often talked about the scary Halloween incident over the next five years, especially when 31st October loomed and none of them ever meddled with the occult again.

Then, in 1984, Emma met Roy, who she regarded as the ideal man of her dreams. He was tall and blond with expressive sky-blue eyes. She introduced him to all her friends and, by the summer of 1985, she was engaged to him and living in his flat, eagerly looking forward to marriage.

But Emma's boyfriend gradually underwent a drastic change of personality and she started to see a repulsive side of him that she had never suspected. He frequently came home drunk and ordered Emma to make him something for supper. His behaviour deteriorated and he ended up throwing a coffee table at her. She left him for a week and stayed at her sister's house but Roy found out where she was and continually telephoned her, begging and pleading for her to return. She finally consented, in the hope that he would clean up his act but his drunken antics continued. One night, as Roy was lying beside Emma in bed, she noticed that the hair at the crown of his head had red roots. She had assumed that he was a natural blond but he confessed that he hated his red hair and had asked his sister to dye it for the last two years. Emma told him it didn't matter what colour his hair was and she persuaded him to let his normal colour return. Roy agreed and, six months later, Emma got the shock of her life when they were having an argument one night.

She was pleading with him to give up drinking, when he suddenly turned violent and slapped her across the face. Grabbing a large knife from the kitchen, he threatened to shut her up for good. He snarled and screwed up his eyes with unbridled hatred and, in a flash, Emma remembered seeing that same face, five years previously, in the mirror on that eventful Halloween night. She was so startled by the chilling sense of deja vu, that she fled the house and went back to her parents. The police were called out and Roy was arrested. Emma vowed never to return to her violent ex-boyfriend and married someone else. To this day, she believes that the spirits warned her about Roy on that memorable night and probably saved her life as a result.

And finally, a short but pleasant tale to round off our trilogy of Halloween ghost stories. This true incident occurred on Tuesday 31st October 1995, in Widnes. Brandon, a 5-year-old boy, came down from his bedroom giggling. His bemused mother, Kirsty, asked her son why he was chuckling and his answer made her blood run cold.

'Grandad's got a Sooty puppet.' Brandon was grinning from ear to ear but became puzzled by his mother's grim reaction.

Kirsty's father had died seven years previously, two years before Brandon's birth, and her father-in-law had died ten years ago. So Kirsty at first assumed that Brandon was talking about an imaginary character, as he had a vivid imagination and often said Mickey Mouse or Spiderman were upstairs in his room, playing with his toys.

But when Kirsty went up to her son's room she was shocked to see an old yellow glove puppet of Sooty, the character she used to watch on TV in the 1970s, when she was a child. Then, with a shudder, Kirsty recalled that her father had bought her an identical Sooty glove puppet one Christmas in her childhood. The only other explanation was that Brandon had taken the puppet from a friend but she doubted that explanation. So she quizzed her son about the puppet and he told her that an old man had appeared in his room, earlier that day. He said that the man called him 'chuck', which was the name Kirsty's dad called her when she was small. Brandon then carried on excitedly,

'Oh yeah, Mum. He said you should hang apples up for me.'

Brandon's comments really struck a chord and jogged his mum's memories. When she was a child, her father and mother always tied cotton threads to the stalks of apples and hung them in the doorway. Kirsty and her brothers would then try to bite the apples with their hands behind their backs.

Inspired by these nostalgic reminiscences, Kirsty took Brandon to the greengrocer's and bought some apples and a big pumpkin to hollow out and make into a lantern. That evening, Kirsty and her husband hung up some of the apples from and challenged Brandon to bite them, without using his hands. Then his dad put four or five apples in his son's inflatable paddling pool and filled it with water. He and Brandon then competed with Kirsty in a duck-apple competition. Brandon really enjoyed the Halloween customs and his dad wanted to tell him a ghost story before bed but Kirsty felt he might have nightmares, so he was put to bed after she had read him an innocuous 'Mister Men' story.

At around 1am, Kirsty picked up a solitary green apple floating in the paddling pool in the garden and took it into the kitchen. She noticed something embedded in it. Her husband saw it too and complained that it was dangerous to put coins into the apples – Brandon could have choked. Kirsty protested that she hadn't put it in and started to prise out the coin. She was confronted with a real 'blast from the past'. The coin was one which they had not seen since they were children. It was a threepenny bit – an old brass-coloured pre-decimal coin, equivalent to three old pence. They were both at a loss to explain how the antiquated coin had found its way into the apple but Kirsty suspected that her dad was the culprit, as he had always hidden a threepenny coin in an apple for her on duck-apple night. Of course, Kirsty didn't dare tell her husband about her suspicions, in case he thought she was crazy.

About a month later, Kirsty was leafing through her old family album one rainy afternoon in a nostalgic mood, when Brandon came over and started to study the old photographs. The boy's face suddenly lit up as he pointed to an untitled picture of Kirsty's father and casually rremarked 'That's Grandad. He comes to my room!'

Sometimes they come back

If we accept that some ghosts are manifestations of spirits who have returned from that shady borderland beyond death, we have to ask, why do they come back? Thousands of people die each minute and it would seem that only a minute percentage return, possibly because of unfinished business or because the deceased person's spirit refuses to leave a loved one, whereas the majority go on into the great unknown. The following stories are about the ones who come back.

One sunny July afternoon in 1995, a 60-year-old woman named Carol sat in an oak-panelled cafe in Chester, serenely gazing through the wide front window at the panoramic street scene outside.

In the midst of the milling crowds, Carol noticed a couple in their early twenties stolling by holding hands. The girl was slim, tall and quite tanned with long, straight blond hair and a round face. Her young man was as tall as her and was foreign in appearance, possibly Spanish or Italian, having ebony-coloured hair. Walking closely behind them, with his head bowed, as if in a miserable mood, was a man of a similar age with short blond hair, sporting a white, Calvin Klein tee shirt and a pair of dark shorts.

Anyway, Carol thought nothing more of the trio as she sipped her cappuccino. About an hour later, the couple walked past the cafe window again, trailed by the young man in the white tee shirt, still looking gloomy on such a bright summer's day. The couple crossed over to look in the window of a bookshop opposite the cafe. All three entered the shop and, about ten minutes later, the couple emerged and re-crossed the street to go into the cafe where Carol had been casually observing them. This time there was no sign of their long-faced friend.

They sat at a table near Carol and ordered something to eat and a couple of soft drinks. Carol smiled at the man and woman, then curiously inquired where their friend was.

The blond girl returned a puzzled stare, so Carol proceeded to describe the man she had seen shadowing them. The girl reacted to the description by clutching her boyfriend's hand. He, too, seemed very anxious all of a sudden.

The girl, a Liverpool University student named Corinne, said that her previous boyfriend, Ian, had committed suicide a year ago, after breaking up with her when she met Anthony, her Spanish boyfriend. Corinne added that Ian had once worked in the bookshop opposite the cafe and Carol, who has had many psychic experiences over the years, felt a cold chill. The man in the white tee shirt following the couple, had obviously been Ian's ghost. Corinne said that she herself had seen Ian's ghost walking behind her one night, shortly after he had committed suicide by hanging himself.

There is a chilling epilogue to this incident. In the summer of 1997, Carol was walking up Liverpool's Church Street when she spotted Corinne and Anthony coming out of a Miss Selfridge store and there, following the couple, was the same, sad, fair-haired man in his tee shirt and shorts. Carol was so shocked at the sight of the vivid apparition, that she became rooted to the spot, unable to greet the couple, who disappeared into the crowds of shoppers.

In 1990 at Orford in Warrington, there was a chilling report of a solid-looking apparition of a man who returned from the grave on three occasions.

In November 1990, a 69-year-old man named Ken died after suffering a cardiac arrest. His son, Duggie, who lived with his father, was heartbroken but to his live-in girlfiend, Helen, Ken's death was a case of good riddance. In the seven months Ken had known Helen, he had made it perfectly clear that he regarded his prospective daughter-in-law as a two-timing gold-digger. Duggie couldn't understand his father's animosity towards the girl he loved and the hostility had been the cause of many heated rows between father and son.

Just half an hour before Ken died of a heart attack, he had warned his son:

'That girl's no good for you. I've seen her type before. She's using you.'

About a week after Ken's funeral, Duggie awoke one night with an unbearable thirst. He left his bed, where Helen was sleeping soundly and went out onto the landing to switch on the downstairs hall light. At this point, Duggie thought he heard a something downstairs. It sounded like a cough and the noise startled him. He crept downstairs and glanced about the hall. All the doors were closed and nothing seemed amiss. He took a chilled bottle of mineral water from the fridge and poured himself a glass. As he sipped his drink, a cold shudder coursed through his body and he somehow knew it was not merely the effect of the drink. He noticed that his arms were covered with goosebumps. He left the kitchen and felt compelled to cross the hall until he reached the parlour door. Duggie suddenly felt very uneasy, it was almost as if he could sense something unearthly behind the door. As he opened it, the stench of stale tobacco smoke greeted his nostrils. He immediately recognised the aroma of Golden Virginia, his father's favourite tobacco.

Peering into the darkness of the parlour, he experienced a mounting sense of fear swelling from the pit of his stomach, as he noticed the outline of somebody sitting on a straight-backed chair. He was unable to switch on the light as he remembered that the bulb had gone but, by the light from the hall, he gradually discerned his father staring at him with a mournful expression.

'Dad?' gasped Duggie, 'Is that you?'

'Get rid of her son. She's no good,' a faint voice replied from the shadows as the apparition seemed to melt away.

'Dad...' Duggie ventured warily into the dismal room to find that the old chair was now empty. He went back upstairs in a daze and found Helen awake.

'Who were you talking to on the phone?' she asked.

'Oh, nobody. I was just yawning.'

'Have you been smoking?' She could smell the tobacco odour too.

'No, just go back to sleep.'

For the remainder of that night, he was troubled with recurrent dreams featuring the vision of his father.

Three weeks later, Duggie got a part-time job driving a fork-lift truck in a wooden pallet factory. One evening, at 7.30, he was having a short coffee break at the warehouse, in a dimly-lit storage area, when he encountered something which was to haunt him for the rest of his life. A solitary figure came walking towards him down the long aisle between the towering stacks of pallets. At first, he thought it was his workmate, Bob, but he soon saw that it was actually his late father. He felt his stomach churn as the vision of his dad marched silently towards him.

'Dad, I don't believe it!' Duggie muttered and stepped back in shock. He became so terrified of the approaching apparition, that he called out for his friend Bob at the top of his voice.

The ghostly figure halted, twenty feet from Duggie, who was now a trembling wreck.

'Go home now,' said the ghost, its mouth seeming to move in slow motion. Seconds later, it vanished. Duggie was so petrified, that he couldn't even walk through the space where the spectre had stood.

'What's up, mate?' asked Bob as he ran into the aisle, in response to Duggie's cry.

'Nothing,' Duggie answered, then rushed headlong past his friend, saying, 'I'm going home, I'm not well.'

He arrived home to find Helen with a stranger; a man wearing a blue ski hat. The two of them were in the living room searching through the sideboard drawers. In her hand, she held a copy of Ken's will and the stranger had Duggie's credit cards in his gloved hand. Duggie called the police immediately. Meanwhile, Helen and her partner in crime fled from the house. They were later apprehended and identified as an estranged couple who were wanted for perpetrating a string of professional confidence tricks. Duggie was devastated when he learned that Helen was a seasoned con artist, out to rob the fortune his father was rumoured to have stashed away in the house. Then he recalled how his father's ghost had warned him and advised him to go home.

He was so shaken by the two encounters with his dead father that he sought psychiatric help. Psychoanalysis elicited nothing beyond the fact that he was a normal, down-to-earth person, who was not prone to hallucinations. In fact, all of Duggie's friends regard him as a fairly unimaginative fellow, with his feet planted firmly on the ground.

In 1991, he met and married a hospital nurse named Lucy, a hardworking and trustworthy girl. At the wedding ceremony, Duggie had a last glimpse of his late father. At the back of the church, he saw him smiling, as if he was elated that his son had found the right girl at last. Moments later he was gone.

That was the last time Duggie set eyes on his concerned father, who returned from the grave to save his only son from a deceitful woman.

The wail of the banshee

From the many years I have put into researching paranormal incidents, I have come to accept that, besides the known dimensions of space and time, there are other realms in our universe, of which we are entirely ignorant. Furthermore, I would hazard a guess that these undiscovered domains, next door to our dimension, are inhabited by various strange life-forms, ranging from the amorphous, to the humanoid. These 'extra-dimensionals' or, 'ultra-terrestrials', may be responsible for the ancient, worldwide myths of elves, fairies and many other legendary creatures, now forgotten and filed away under 'folklore'.

Those who consider that the notion of unknown, exotic aliens living in close proximity to us is nonsense, only have to reflect on the peculiar life-forms inhabiting our own world. Imagine what Captain Cook would have made of the surreal-looking kangaroo during his exploration of Australia. The existence of such an animal, carrying its young in a pocket-like pouch, was entirely unexpected. Another comical-looking animal, which eluded zoologists until 1937, was the giant panda of northern China. In 1912, another unusual creature was discovered when a pilot was forced to make an emergency landing on an island off Malaya. He was confronted with a living dinosaur; a three metre long monitor lizard, now known as the Komodo Dragon. This fearsome, 135-kilogram animal has a long tail and enormous jaws which can kill a man.

Closer to home, on this very page in fact, there are hordes of grotesque, microscopic monsters, known as dust mites, prowling across the paper avariciously munching on the tiny detached flakes of your skin. These minute creatures look like some nightmarish, bug-eyed monsters from an Hieronymous Bosch painting under the electron microscope but, thankfully, because they live on another scale of reality, we are never aware of them crawling about in the carpet and in our beds.

Similarly, could there be undiscovered species of weird but

intelligent creatures living alongside us in a parallel dimension, perhaps secretly observing us and occasionally meddling in human affairs? Would this hypothesis explain poltergeists, the mysterious 'greys' allegedly responsible for global abductions, angels and perhaps even some UFO sightings? In recent years, many respected researchers into the paranormal, including ufologists such as Jaques Vallee and John Keel, have presented convincing conjectures suggesting that some unknown agency outside space and time has been preying on the collective subconscious of mankind for many millenia, manifesting itself as angels, demons, visions, fairies, spirits, will o' the wisp and various other supernatural guises. In this chapter, we will take a look at one of these sinister entities: the banshee.

The banshee is one of the most well-known figures of Irish folklore. The name is derived from the Irish Gaelic 'bean sidhe', meaning 'woman of the fairies'. According to tradition, the banshee's mournful cry is said to fortell death. The banshee is described as having long, straight white or red hair which covers her face and she combs her hair as she wails outside the family home of the person who is about to die. Fortunately, the person who is about to pass away never hears or sees the banshee and, once the death has taken place, the crying ceases and the eerie apparition instantly vanishes. Although we are living in the modern hi-tech age of computers, genetic-engineering and space travel, it seems, from the following cases, that the chilling Celtic mourner is still doing her rounds and not only in Ireland; she has also been active, of late, in Cheshire.

In Ellesmere Port, in the autumn of 1997, Sarah Wayne, a 50-year-old housewife, was sitting up late one Saturday night, waiting for her 18-year-old daughter, Cheryl, to return from a nightclub. Sarah hadn't been keen on her teenaged daughter going out to the club but Cheryl had argued that she was old enough to look after herself and added that Liam, the boy she was after, went to the club on a Saturday night.

Sarah's husband, Derek, was in Nottingham driving a heavy-goods vehicle to a depot. He was very protective towards his only daughter and certainly would have done his utmost to prevent her from going to the nightclub.

The time was 2.30am and still there was no sign of Cheryl, so her mother dimmed the lights in the parlour and peeped through the net curtains at the deserted street outside. A wind was starting to stir and a cluster of dried leaves swirled by on the pavement. Sarah scanned both ends of the road for twenty minutes but Cheryl was nowhere to be seen. Around 3am, Mrs Wayne was anxiously sipping a cup of tea in the living room, watching the BBC News 24 service on the muted TV. At around 3.30, she fell into a light sleep but a sound woke her up minutes later. Startled, she opened her eyes and saw Cheryl walk past the living room in the hall sobbing with her platinum blond hair in a mess. It straggled down in front of her face.

'Cheryl! What's wrong, love? Where have you been?' Mrs Wayne bolted from the armchair and followed Cheryl, who had headed straight to the kitchen. Sarah assumed that her distraught daughter had been rejected by Liam at the club but, when she walked into the kitchen, the woman got the shock of her life. The room was empty; Cheryl was nowhere to be seen.

Then came the sounds of a yale key rattling in the front door. Cheryl came in with her friend, Jacqueline, laughing and talking about the boys they'd danced with. Her long blond hair was piled up in a bun on her head and she wore a bright red mini skirt and a white sleeveless top. The figure her mother had pursued to the kitchen had its hair draped over its face and seemed to be wearing black clothes. Sarah Wayne suddenly realised that she had mistaken a weeping ghost for her daughter and her heart skipped a beat. She told Cheryl and her friend about the weird apparition and the three of them became so jittery, they all refused to go into the kitchen until dawn broke.

Around breakfast time, a policeman and woman called at the house to inform Sarah of her husband's death in Nottingham. He had left the cab of his lorry at 3.30am. that morning and suffered a fatal heart attack. The death took place at the precise time that the crying ghost had walked through the hallway. Was the apparition just a so-called 'open-eye' dream of Mrs Wayne's, who had just woken up, or was it a banshee? Mrs Wayne believes it was a banshee and was so unnerved by the experience, that she later moved from the house and now lives in Bebington.

The second report of a banshee comes from three witnesses. It all began in the early hours of a Wednesday morning in August 1998, when Freda Piers, a 44-year-old housewife of Saltney, Chester, had difficulty sleeping. Freda usually had no trouble getting to sleep but on this balmy morning at 2am, she became restless and insomnia steadily began to set in. She therefore left her snoring husband and went down to the kitchen to make a coffee. She turned on the radio and for about a minute she listened to Magic 1548, a Liverpool-based station. She was just about to turn the radio off, when the disc-jockey, Jon Jessop, urged listeners to go and look out of their windows to see if there was any sign of a lost, snow-white terrier named Brandy, because its owner was frantic. Freda dimmed the lights, parted the blinds and gazed out at the moonlit close. She heard a low howling sound which sent a shiver down her spine. The DJ then said that the terrier had been lost in northern Liverpool, so Freda realised that there was no hope of the dog being outside her house in Saltney. Nevertheless, she took a quick peep through the gaps in the blinds and saw a hooded figure in black, standing across the road. The figure looked like a monk wearing a black habit and cowl. What's more, it seemed to be the source of the uncanny weeping and was staring up at the bedroom window of the house opposite. Red curtains were drawn in this window and a faint bulb burned behind them.

Freda telephoned her best friend, Eunice, who lived next door to the house where the strange figure was lurking. After some twenty or so rings, a bleary-eyed and grumpy Eunice answered her phone and Freda told her about the figure in black standing in the neighbouring garden on the lawn. Eunice took her cordless phone to the window and looked out. She told Freda that an old, white-haired woman was looking up at next door's window with a sorrowful but demented look and she appeared to be crying. Eunice was so frightened at the sight of the deranged old woman, that she hung up on Freda, dialled the police and shook her husband awake. Her husband, Kevin, reluctantly hauled himself out of bed and also took a look out of the window. He, too, saw the eccentric old woman in black. He opened the bedroom window, despite his frightened wife's pleas not to and shouted down to her,

'What's wrong, love?'

The creepy-looking woman failed to reply and continued staring up at next door's window and started making a blood-curdling howling noise.

Freda, meanwhile, was attempting to awaken her husband, Sam, to tell him about the crazy old woman on the other side of the close.

A police car zoomed to the scene with its roof-light flashing. Eunice and Kevin were momentarily distracted and, when they glanced back at the lawn, the nocturnal visitor had inexplicably vanished, literally in the blinking of an eye. Two policemen rushed from the squad car flashing the beams of their high-powered torches across the garden in search of the mysterious figure. Eunice felt so stupid and confused at the woman's disappearance, that she withdrew from the window and pulled her husband back too. However, seconds later, burning with curiosity, she chanced a peep through the net curtains and the blinding beam of a torch singled out her face at the window. Eunice had no option but to lean out and identify herself as the person who had rung the police.

The police listened patiently, then knocked on the front door of Eunice's neighbour. A middle-aged man came to the door not long afterwards and invited them in. About fifteen minutes later, an ambulance roared into the close. The ambulancemen hurried to the house and were admitted by the policemen. By now, Freda, Eunice, and their husbands, were standing on the pavement outside the house which was the focus of all the activity. Eunice and her husband recalled that an Irish couple, the O'Briens, had recently moved into it.

Some time later, the covered body of Mrs O'Brien was brought out to the ambulance on a stretcher. Afterwards, Freda and Eunice learned that Mrs O'Brien had died in her sleep. Her husband, Pat, had woken at 2am to the sounds of someone crying outside. He had tried to awaken his wife, Philomena, but she failed to respond. Mr O'Brien panicked when he felt her neck and could find no carotid pulse. She also felt cold and Mr O'Brien slowly realised his wife was dead.

Mr O'Brien claims that his own mother's death, 25 years earlier, was foreshadowed by the wailing of a banshee and has no difficulty accepting that a banshee cried for his late wife, in the early hours of that warm August morning.

These banshee reports are just a couple of examples of the many cases I've looked into and most of the accounts are difficult to rationalize as hallucinations or outright lies, given the calibre of the witnesses. In many instances, the ghostly mourner was seen by several, unrelated observers simultaneously, which surely rules any subjective mirage in the mind of the witnesses. A classic case in point, is the doomed Piper Alpha Oil Platform Disaster in 1988. Derek Ellington, a rig fitter, and many of his workmates on the oil platform, heard an eerie screeching noise which sounded like a woman crying hysterically. Less than a minute later, an enormous fireball engulfed the rig and 160 workers perished. Derek Ellington was one of the lucky survivors who were plucked from the icy waters of the North Sea. He was later asked to describe the strange sound which seemed to be some portent of the disaster and he recalled it as being 'like the wailing of a banshee'.

The Winsford Vampire

When I was a child, adults confidently reassured me that vampires, such as the legendary Dracula, do not and never did exist. Today I know they were wrong to dismiss the bloodsuckers. Believe me, vampires do exist but there are two varieties of them nowadays; fake and genuine. Firstly, there are cults in several major cities, notably San Francisco and London, in which members drink each other's blood and the blood of sacrificed people and animals. Not a very sensible idea in the AIDS era but a cursory browse of the Internet will list hundreds of these vampiric sects. Many of the blood-drinkers undoubtedly indulge in this type of vampirism for erotic reasons but, throughout history, from the days of the ancient Egyptians to the present, there have been many well-documented reports of real vampires attacking and subduing victims.

We don't have to go back thousands of years to examine reports of these strange beings, because there have been several vampire alerts in modern times and they are still being reported today.

On 16th April 1922, a man was admitted to London's Charing Cross Hospital with a strange, deep wound in his neck. All he could remember was that he had been turning a corner off Coventry Street, when he felt an agonizing stabbing sensation in his neck which caused him to pass out. He saw no attacker, so the police had nothing to go on. A few hours later, another man was brought into the hospital with a similar wound. He, too, had felt a sharp pain in his neck before losing consciousness, at the very same turning off Coventry Street near Piccadilly Circus. This second victim was also unable to give a description of his assailant because there had been no one within twenty feet of him. Incredibly, a third patient was later taken to the hospital and he, too, had a deep neck wound which he had received at the same spot.

The People newspaper covered the strange story and rumours of a vampire, at large in the West End, spread like wildfire. Alas, the invisible Coventry Street attacker was never apprehended by Scotland Yard but the case has all the hallmarks of a true vampire assault. You see, contrary to popular belief, vampires do not turn into bats and fly off in search of victims; that was the invention of Bram Stoker, who created the anti-hero, Dracula, in his 1897 novel. From the data we have on actual vampire attacks, it would seem that these strange, bloodthirsty beings have the ability to 'teleport' themselves about, either in physical form, or by somehow projecting their wraith, or astral body, to the victim's home. Furthermore, the genuine vampire rarely bites the victim to imbibe blood. Instead, it usually draws off the very life-energy of the victim, leaving him physically ill and mentally exhausted.

In fact, the symptoms of a subtle vampire assault, are identical to a condition that is becoming increasingly prevalent in the civilized world: ME, short for myalgic encephalomyelitis. This is a benign but debilitating (and often long-lasting) condition, which allegedly occurs out of the blue, causing headaches, weakness, muscular pain, extreme fatigue and even fever. Over 150,000 people in Britain are affected by this puzzling condition and, for some reason, most of the sufferers are women. The medical authorities still cannot agree amongst themselves about the nature of ME. Some doctors think the condition is psychosomatic, while others believe the syndrome has a link with the coxsackieviruses in the human body. Whatever the cause, the strange, incapacitating condition is reaching epidemic proportions world-wide.

No one had even heard of ME in 1970 but, in the summer of that year, Judith, a 19-year-old Winsford girl, was stricken with ME-like symptoms. A doctor examined the teenager and initially diagnosed flu but the girl returned a week later, accompanied by her mother. She was very pale and lethargic and had a number of purple marks on her neck and breasts. The GP identified the discolorations as 'love bites' and concluded that the girl was suffering from a form of glandular fever which is commonly spread from french kissing. However, Judith's mother went on to tell the doctor about her daughter's screaming fits in the dead of night and the strange lucid nightmares which haunted her sleep. Judith's own accounts of these night terrors resulted in her being referred to a psychiatrist, Dr Dwerringwood. She told him that once midnight arrived, she felt a sinister, cold presence invading her bedroom. Then, a young man in black would appear at the foot of her bed, leering at her as she lay paralysed with fear. Asked if she could identify him, Judith claimed it was a foreign-looking art student from her neighbourhood named Lazzlo, who, although attractive, had a creepy presence about him. She then gave details about the first 'assault' in her bedroom.

'I was just nodding off, when I felt a cold hand stroking my breasts. I opened my eyes and the room was in darkness but someone was on top of me and he was kissing and biting my neck. I was so frightened, I couldn't move or cry out. I closed my eyes and hoped I was just having a nightmare but, when I opened them, he was still there. From the light of the lampost shining into my bedroom, I saw his face. It was Lazzlo.'

The young man in question, Lazzlo Ordog, was a 23-year-old Hungarian art student. He was quite tall; over six feet in height, with olive skin and black, slicked-back hair and a lively pair of dark brown, probing eyes.

Dr Dwerringwood quizzed Judith about her relationship with her father, as he suspected he might be the nocturnal culprit but he had died several years before. The psychiatrist therefore asked if any uncles or male relatives were staying at Judith's house. Only her 6-year-old brother, Graham, who had no time for girls.

Then came the bizarre twist in this intriguing case. Another girl in the neighbourhood was also referred to Dwerringwood. The girl, Zara, had just turned sixteen and her body displayed the same cluster of love-bites on the neck and breasts. She also exhibited the same apathetic symptoms as Judith and, stranger still, this girl also nervously related how, on some nights, a 'ghost' got into bed with her and tried to have sex with her. Dwerringwood asked Zara to describe this ghost and her descriptions matched Judith's in every detail. The apparition was handsome but spooky, with black hair and penetrating eyes. The psychiatrist also suggested that perhaps it had been a nightmare but the girl insisted she had been awake throughout the nightly ordeals, which stretched back months. He then asked if the man ressembled anyone she knew. She revealed that she had spotted someone who was identical to him. Zara didn't know his name but she knew which street his lodgings were in – the very same street where Lazzlo Ordog lived.

The police were powerless to quiz the Hungarian on the strength of such a bizarre testimony but Dwerringwood decided, out of curiosity, to break with protocol and pay a visit to Lazzlo. The landlady who ran the small boarding house admitted the psychiatrist into the hall and summoned Mr Ordog. The student crept silently down the stairs and, with a furtive half-smile on his face, gave the disquieting impression that he had been expecting Dwerringwood to call. The psychiatrist introduced himself and asked if he could speak to him in private for a few minutes. The student simply nodded and beckoned him up to his attic quarters.

Lazzlo was evidently using the room as his studio. There were several canvasses propped up on easels. All were of female nudes and most were incomplete but Dwerringwood was intrigued to see two finished watercolours lying side by side in a corner of the room. The subjects were two girls who bore an uncanny resemblance to Judith and Zara. Dwerringwood asked who had posed for the two paintings but Lazzlo claimed he had painted the girls from imagination.

The psychiatrist got straight to the point and told Lazzlo how he was the bogeyman haunting the dreams of two troubled teenagers. He added that both girls had identified Lazzlo as the nocturnal visitor and then asked him if he had any theories as to why they might be dreaming of him.

The Hungarian suddenly couldn't maintain eye-contact with the psychiatrist and, after shrugging off Dwerringwood's question, he busied himself with the arrangement of his paint tubes. Then, in an irritated manner he blurted out,

'Girls are crazy!'.

The psychiatrist now felt very uneasy being alone with the art student and decided to leave. As he reached the door, Lazzlo turned to him and asked,

'What do you think of the girls' stories? Do you believe them?'

Dwerringwood felt the hairs stand up on the back of his neck. He didn't turn around. Instead he left, mumbling,

'I don't know.'

When he returned home, Dwerringwood found his cat lying dead on the doorstep. There were no signs of physical injury on the cat's body, so he took it to the vet, who was a friend of his. The vet could not establish the cause of death and the psychiatrist felt his pet's death was somehow connected to the sinister Hungarian painter. On the following night, as he was watching the late news on TV, the mirror above his fireplace split in half with a loud crack. He could not explain the cracked mirror and later that same night, when he retired to bed, he distinctly caught a glimpse of a man's silhouette standing at the top of his stairs. The shadow-like figure vanished a split-second after Dwerringwood glanced at it, but it looked like Lazzlo Ordog's outline. He knew he had not imagined the figure, even though its transient appearance flew in the face of reason.

Dwerringwood never told his fiancee, Glynis, about the strange incidents or about the mysterious Hungarian but, one night they were lying in bed together, when she woke up choking. She felt a pair of powerful, ice-cold hands wrapped around her throat, throttling her. As soon as she managed to scream out, the strangling sensation ceased. She was so sure there was an attacker in the bedroom, that she jumped out of bed and rushed to switch on the light, but there was nobody there.

Dwerringwood racked his brains, wondering what he was up against. He was a man of scientific rationality and he felt out of his depth tackling the menacing Lazzlo Ordog. One afternoon, a bizarre thought dawned on him: what if the Hungarian was some sort of vampire? It was a far-fetched idea but the more he thought about him, the less ludicrous his theory seemed. He obtained two copies of the Bible and bought three small crucifixes. He left one copy of the Bible in Judith's bedroom and the other in Zara's bedroom. He also gave the girls a crucifix each and told them to wear it when they went to bed.

Dwerringwood wore the third crucifix on a chain about his neck and, when he went to bed, he turned off the lamp and settled down ready to sleep. Then a low gruff voice, seething with hate, whispered in his ear:

'I'll break your neck one day.' The voice sounded as if it came from someone standing at the bedside.

For as long as Judith and Zara wore the crucifixes and left the Bibles in their rooms, they enjoyed a quiet night's sleep, regained their zeal for living and the purple contusions quickly faded from their bodies.

Some time later, Dwerringwood went to the lodging house to interview Lazzlo again. This time, he carried a Bible and wore his crucifix, ready to confront the creepy young man but Lazzlo had left. The landlady said he had moved out during the night, without leaving a forwarding address.

Dwerringwood's experiment with the Bibles and crucifixes seemed to do the job and yet, for many years afterwards, he struggled to rationalize the whole vampire episode and wondered if it had just been a case of hysteria, autosuggestion or coincidence.

Curiously, in October 1991, there was a haunting reported in Winsford. In the very house where the teenager Judith had lived in the 1970s, a young woman awoke one morning at 4am and was confronted by a man in black, with his arms stretched out, floating close to the ceiling directly above her bed. The woman was naturally terrified by the floating phantom and she hid under the covers, quaking with fear. She summoned enough courage to have another peep at the ceiling and found that the black-clad figure had vanished. Was Lazzlo on the prowl again?

According to the acupuncturists of ancient China, the health of a person depended on the life-force ch'i. If ch'i did not flow smoothly and harmoniously through the body, physical and mental sickness were said to result. Ch'i was regarded as the very essence of the soul, circulating under the skin through a series of specific channels known as meridians. Recent scientific research has proved beyond doubt that the human body is buzzing with electric fields and, furthermore, any interference with these fields can have serious medical repercussions. It has been proven, for example, that children living in close proximity to electric pylons and substations, are more likely to develop leukaemia because strong electromagnetic fields have a detrimental effect on the body's immune system. Perhaps this is how Lazzlo and others like him prey on their victims; by sapping the very essence of their life-energy, or ch'i.

For all we know, parasitic vampires may be at large at this very moment in our society, draining the energy of their unsuspecting victims. Would this explain the explosion in recent years of ME cases? Have you been feeling run-down lately?

The Cuddington doppelganger

In July 1994, a 17-year-old Californian girl, Mercedes Phillips, visited her English penpal Tanya Owens, in Cuddington, which lies just a couple of miles west of Northwich.

It was the first time Mercedes had actually met her friend, although the two girls, who were both the same age, had corresponded on an almost daily basis via the Internet. However, Tanya felt somewhat inferior to her trans-Atlantic friend. The slim-figured Mercedes was almost 6 feet tall, with long, natural blond hair and a genuine golden tan. She had sparkling sky-blue eyes, a little snub nose and perfect, pearly-white teeth. The petite Tanya had shoulder-length, fuzzy red hair, a face dotted with freckles and wore a brace on her teeth. Despite their obvious superficial differences, the two penpals got on very well together. A day after her arrival, Tanya took her jet-lagged friend to Delamere Forest and showed her many of the rural scenes and sights of local historic interest. During the tour, a boy on a mountain bike almost ran into Tanya, as he came careering down a lane. It turned out to be a 16-year-old from Weaversham named Dylan. Tanya's heart fluttered when she saw him, as she'd had her eyes on him for almost a year but he never seemed interested in her. However, Dylan was certainly interested in the ravishing Californian.

'Wow. Who are you?'

'Mercedes,' she replied, smiling at the boy.

'Aren't you Dylan? I've seen you around.' Tanya said. She lacked the confidence to smile at the boy because of her brace.

Dylan was so bewitched with the Californian, that he didn't reply but just gave a mock chuckle and said,

'Mercedes? That's a car.'

Merceded giggled and told him,

'It's Spanish for mercy, but yeah, my Dad was a car freak.'

Tanya's heart was in turmoil. She couldn't endure the boy of her dreams being so spellbound by her friend, so she walked on, dragging Mercedes along by the elbow.

Dylan cycled after the girls until they reached Tanya's home. Before Mercedes went into the house, Dylan summoned up enough guts to ask her out. She said she already had a boyfriend back home in San Diego.

'I'll be your new boyfriend then.' Dylan suggested and awaited a reply. Mercedes just smiled and waved before entering the house. Tanya glared back at Dylan, then slammed the door behind her.

Over the next couple of days, wherever Tanya and Mercedes went, Dylan would follow like a shadow. Then one night, Mercedes confessed that she thought Dylan was cute and handsome. She also announced that she had split with her boyfriend back in San Diego three months previously. Tanya tried to dissuade her from getting involved with him to no effect and, within a week, Mercedes and Dylan were walking about holding hands and gazing into each other's eyes. The more Mercedes got to know the boy from Weaversham, the more she felt they had in common. He was a Libran like her and loved poetry, she was a closet poet. They were both into astronomy and believed in reincarnation. In fact, Dylan swore he felt as if he had met Mercedes in some previous life in Ancient Greece!

Tanya was naturally devastated and, in the end, resigned herself to the fact that Dylan wasn't interested in her. However, she secretly hoped he would fall in love with her one day; perhaps next summer, when her teeth would be brace-free.

Mercedes had to return to America in the middle of August and she pleaded for Dylan to visit her soon in California. However, he had five brothers and sisters and his parents were barely able to make ends meet, never mind send their son off on holiday to the United States. Dylan was too proud to say that he didn't have the money for the flight and promised he would visit her soon. He didn't even have the money to travel to Manchester Airport to see her off and, on that day, he thought his world had ended when she left. He revisited all the places where they had strolled hand in hand and inwardly cried. At least he had her home and e-mail address. But, when he searched his untidy bedroom, he discovered, to his horror, that he had lost the scrap of paper with the addresses on. He visited Tanya but she said she'd lost

Mercedes' e-mail address too. She was lying of course; she didn't want him to have anything to do with the American.

Dylan panicked and frantically searched his bedroom once more but couldn't find the piece of paper. He called at Tanya's house again but her mother answered the door and told him to stop calling for her. As he walked away, he caught sight of the jealous girl peeping through the blinds of her bedroom window.

Coincidentally, Mercedes had accidently left Dylan's address on a piece of paper in Tanya's home in England and, when she realised this, she e-mailed her friend and asked her to send it over the Internet. But Tanya lied and said that she didn't have his address and that he was already dating another girl. Mercedes cried when she read Tanya's e-mail. She wondered how Dylan could be so cold when she thought they'd had something so special.

The lovelorn Dylan, meanwhile, continued to roam about on his bike, reminiscing about the wonderful days he'd spent with Mercedes. She'd been the first proper girlfriend he'd ever had and now it was all over. One Sunday afternoon, at 4 'o' clock, a fortnight after Mercedes' departure, he was cycling along a country lane which was covered in autumn leaves. This lane, on the northern peripheries of Cuddington, ran through a quiet, wooded area which had been one of their favourite spots, where they had made so many promises to each other. Lost in his emotional recollections, Dylan suddenly noticed a figure approaching down the lane. His heart missed a beat. It was her – Mercedes!

He braked and, in disbelief, called out her name then dismounted. Mercedes was only fifty feet away but she didn't react. It was as if she hadn't noticed him yet. As she walked along with her head bowed, she seemed very pensive and Dylan suddenly noticed that she was wearing a long white gown of some sort. The lane was covered with dry, ochrous leaves, which rustled loudly under foot as he strode eagerly towards her. Yet the girl didn't make any sound as she walked along. Dylan was completely overjoyed and sighed,

'You're back. I knew you'd come back to me.'

Suddenly, Mercedes wasn't there any more. She had vanished, leaving Dylan rushing towards an empty cold space. He stood there, trying to fathom out what had just occurred. Was he going insane? Was it a ghost? With a mounting sense of dread, he wondered if Mercedes had died and had returned to him as a vision one last time. He was certain it hadn't been an hallucination or some desire image from his despairing mind. The girl had looked so real and solid, yet she had moved silently down the lane. At home, his mother had some good news for him.

'Was this what you were looking for?' she asked and held out a scrap of paper. She had found it in the pocket of her son's jeans, as she was putting them into the washing machine. The ecstatic Dylan grabbed the paper and kissed it. He rushed to his friend's house and e-mailed Mercedes.

She e-mailed him back shortly afterwards and asked him if he was still dating. Dylan was puzzled by the reply but he and Mercedes soon realised that Tanya had fabricated the story to put an end to their relationship. He sent more messages to his American girlfriend and told her about the eerie incident in the lane. She, in turn, told him a strange tale. At 8am on the Sunday, when Dylan had seen her wraith, Mercedes had been intensively imagining she was walking through the woods near Cuddington, in an attempt to ease her depression at the thought of losing her English boyfriend. He said he had encountered the phantom Mercedes around 4pm, not 8am, but his girlfriend explained that her home in California was eight hours behind the time in England so the two incidents were simultaneous. Dylan remembered the white gown, so he asked Mercedes to recall what she had been wearing on that Sunday morning. She told him that she'd worn a white bathrobe, because she had just showered.

What Dylan encountered in the woods that day is open to speculation but I suspect that it was what is known, in occult circles, as a 'doppelganger' or phantasm of the living. These types of apparition are very common and are often mistaken for the ghost of a dead person. Some think that the doppelganger is an etheric counterpart of the physical body which is reserved for the purpose of carrying the soul after death. Occasionally, in times of illness or great distress, it would seem that this ethereal replica is somehow projected or detached from its physical counterpart, through some mysterious process. Many famous people have reported this baffling phenomenon of 'bi-location' in which the doppelganger is projected over considerable distances to materialise in full view of witnesses. In his autobiography, the Irish poet and dramatist WB Yeats writes:

'One afternoon, I was thinking very intently of a fellow student for whom I had a message. In a couple of days I got a letter from a place some hundreds of miles away, where the student was. On the afternoon when I had been thinking so intently, I had suddenly appeared there amid a crowd of people in a hotel and seeming as solid as if in the flesh. My fellow student had seen me but no one else and had asked me to come again, when the people had gone. I had vanished, but had come again in the middle of the night and had given him the message. I myself had no knowledge of either apparition.'

In the 1930s, a similar incident occurred when the Derbyshire-born novelist, John Cowper Powys, told the American writer Theodore Dreiser that he would project himself into the sitting-room of the latter's New York home. Powys caught his train back to a town on the Hudson where he was staying. Dreiser expected some sort of prank but, two hours later, the writer happened to glance up from his book to see Powys standing in the doorway of the sitting-room with a smug smile.

The flabbergasted Dreiser dropped his book and stood up, saying,

'Well, you've kept your word – now tell me how you did it.'

As Dreiser approached Powys, he vanished in an instant. Dreiser immediately rang him to get to the bottom of the mystery. The novelist answered but, depsite his staggered friend's repeated requests asking how he had projected himself into the room, Powys remained tantalizingly tight-lipped right up to his death in 1964.

A rare, but chilling experience, is to come face to face with your own doppelganger. The German poet, Goethe, once met 'himself' coming towards him in the early 19th century. According to European folklore, this should have been an omen of Goethe's imminent death but the poet lived for many years after the disturbing experience. In Victorian times, the doppelganger was known as a 'fetch' and further back in time, in ancient Greece and Egypt, the ghostly double was known as the 'ka', which was envisaged as a vaporous mirror-image of the body, that was attached to the physical body by an invisible cord. This cord was said to snap when a person died.

A word of caution to those of you who intend to experiment in projecting themselves. According to the occultists, when the ka leaves the body empty, it is prey to possession by all manner of evil spirits.

The knowledge

The next intriguing tale, was passed onto me by the relatives of a man who died recently. They requested anonymity, so some names have been changed. I have personally checked the facts of the case and have interviewed many of the people mentioned in the story. I cannot find a rational explanation to account for the incident but I have put forward a few theoretical suggestions.

In the winter of 1990, Joe, a 58-year-old Cestrian, was driving to a friend's house in Macclesfield. He left the A537 and drove down a tree-lined road. The low winter sun flickered through the passing trunks of leafless trees like a strobe and Joe began to experience a strange feeling of dizziness. Joe was an epileptic and he recognised that the rhythm of flickering sunlight flashing through the trees had triggered a seizure. The next thing he knew, he was hurtling down an embankment in his car. Through some miracle, he suffered no harm and was soon back on the road to Macclesfield but, throughout the journey, he felt very strange. A host of peculiar sensations swirled through his head and his brain felt as if it were expanding like a balloon.

Epilepsy is a disease characterized by fits and sudden loss of consciousness. Julius Caesar, Van Gogh, Dostoievski and Byron all suffered and, possibly benefited creatively, from this neurological disorder. In ancient times, epilepsy was known as the 'sacred disease' because many sufferers claimed that during a siezure, their minds transcended normal consciousness to experience a rapturous, timeless and almost religious euphoria, as if they were in communion with the universe or even God.

After his seizure, Joe felt permanently transcended, as if the epileptic fit had somehow elevated his level of consciousness. He found random information, of which he had no previous knowledge, pouring into his mind. Without looking at his watch, he knew precisely where the second finger would be and, before he took a bend in the road, he knew what would be round the corner. He switched on his radio and experienced continual deja vu; he knew that the traffic and weather report would come on next and he could even predict what the newscaster was about to say, word for word. Without warning, Joe's mind suddenly returned to normality. However, the strange, altered state of consciousness returned on several more occasions throughout the next seven years.

One night, Joe was socialising in the pub with his friends in Whitchurch, when one of them decided to enter the quiz for a laugh. Joe and his mates were certainly no intellectuals and never faired well at pub quizzes but, on this particular evening, Joe astounded his friends and himself. As the quizmaster was reading out the questions, he was scribbling away furiously on his entry sheet. No sooner had the quizmaster finished, than Joe handed in his sheet and retained the carbon counterfoil. He had answered all fifty questions correctly, despite the wide range of subjects, about which, he knew nothing. As a result of this sudden brainwave, he won the £100 prize.

On another occasion in Chester, Joe and his wife, Margot, were at the supermarket checkout and, before the girl on the till had even touched their shopping items, Joe informed Margot that their bill would be ninety-five pence higher than the correct total because the checkout girl would accidently scan the bar code of a chocolate mousse twice. On checking the itemised print-out, Margot confirmed his prediction. When questioned about it, he just shrugged.

A couple of weeks later, Margot's mother, who had been suffering from ovarian cancer for some time, was admitted to hospital. Margot was told by a specialist that the tumour was pressing on her bladder, making her incontinent. Joe suddenly stepped forward and gave the doctor detailed constructive suggestions for an operation to make Margot's mother more comfortable. He advised the doctor and a surgeon to divert the woman's ureters – the ducts that convey the urine from the kidneys to the bladder – and perform a urostomy. He went into such detail that the doctor asked him if he had been medically trained. Joe confessed that he did not know how he suddenly knew so much about human anatomy. Amazingly, the surgeon later carried out the operation which Joe had proposed and, although Margot's mother died four years later, the urostomy made her life more comfortable than it would have been.

Joe's inexplicable mental faculty returned on several more occasions. On a holiday in Brittany, he confounded his wife by booking into a hotel in fluent French. This bizarre phenomenon is known as xenolalia, which means speaking a foreign language which one has never learnt. There are many reported cases of xenolalia every year and linguistics experts and psychologists cannot explain its occurrence.

In 1997, some weeks before Joe's sudden death from cardiac arrest, Margot returned home one day and mentioned that she had called at her friend Rita's house, only to find her out. Joe suddenly jumped from his armchair and cried out,

'Rita's husband beats her. He's throttling her now.'

Fully aware of Joe's clairvoyant capabilities, Margot called the police and warned them that a wife-beating was in progress at Rita's home. The police acted on the tip off and, sure enough, Rita had been punched and assaulted by her husband. She had almost been strangled by him at one point in the cowardly attack, just as Joe had claimed.

How can we begin to explain just how this Chester man was able to access so much information and detailed knowledge? I might be wide of the mark but here's my theory:

Throughout the history of human civilisation, there have been individuals who have claimed to be the possessors of arcane knowledge accessed from unknown sources. The Masons, Mystery Schools and various other esoteric groups have professed to possess secrets of the occult. But where did these secret societies get their clandestine information from, in the first place?

Some of the occult knowledge was probably carefully passed down the generations by initiates of the fabled Ancient Wisdom; this being a vast collection of books about cosmic law, the hidden powers of mankind and other mystical matters, supposedly written by the scientists of a super-civilisation in antediluvian times.

But for centuries, occultists have claimed that there is another source of hidden knowledge called the Akashic Records. These records are said to contain data on everything in the universe; every thought and deed of every lifeform, from the beginning of the cosmos, to the present.

The word 'akashic' derives from the Sanskrit 'akasha', meaning the fundamental etheric substance of the universe. The substance is said to fill all space and to link every atom of animate and inanimate matter.

The Akashic Records are therefore like some colossal databank (similar to the Internet but unimaginably more extensive) that contains information about every person and event from the dawn of time to the present day. The Western counterpart of these records would be the Book of Life, where all details about a person's conduct are recorded by their attendant angel.

If you think the notion of vast amounts of information existing in the ether is a bit far-fetched, consider this: gigabytes of data are passing through you and surround you at this very moment as you read these words. TV, satellite and radio signals carrying pictures, music, chat, classified and encoded military information, messages from mobile phones etc, are radiating through your body at the speed of light. This modern day continuous chatter of the electromagnetic spectrum is a good analogy when referring to the Akashic Records. The same thing happens in both cases; unless you know how to tune in and decode the signals around you, they are undetectable and useless.

How then, do you tune in to access the records? Mystics use meditation or visualisation techniques where you simply picture a blank chalkboard and wait for the information you need to appear on it.

Sometimes it would seem that the records are unconsciously accessed at random by people who believe that they have been inspired. For instance, Mozart claimed that he often heard new symphonies playing in his head which didn't seem to be of his making, while Sir Paul McCartney has always maintained that his most popular song, Yesterday, came to him from the depths of his sleep. Many writers and poets, such as Samuel Taylor Coleridge and Charles Dickens, have made the same curious assertions about novels and poems that seemed to have been dictated to them from some invisible author in their unconscious minds. In fact, Coleridge dreamed the whole of his poem 'Kubla Khan' and simply wrote it down in the morning.

Scientists have also made many discoveries in the time-honoured tradition of sleeping on an idea. In 1863, August Kekule, a young

German scientist, experienced such a dream of discovery while dozing on a bus. He dreamt that he was watching chains of carbon and hydrogen atoms slithering about like snakes. Suddenly, one chain formed a type of loop which instantly revealed the molecular structure of benzene. Kekule awoke excited; he had been racking his brain trying to work out the structure of benzene for months and now, all had been revealed to him.

Of course, all the previous cases could be rationalised as the products of a fertile subconscious. However, if the Akashic Records do exist on some higher plane of existence, then the information they contain could often be accessed by more than one person at the same time. Observers have noticed that, when the time is ripe, ideas, inventions and discoveries often appear in different parts of the world simultaneously. For example, in 1900, three scientists in Holland, Germany and Austria Hugo de Vries, Carl Correns, and Erich von Tschermak respectively, independently discovered the laws of genetics on the same day.

In 1876 the same thing happened when Alexander Graham Bell patented the telephone. Another inventor, Elisha Gray, sent a detailed description of his telephone to the US Patent Office a few hours after Bell's. More and more patents for a telephone poured into the office and, within few years, there were some 600 lawsuits over the Bell telephone patents.

But how could something as revolutionary as the telephone be a part of the Akashic Records? Some occultists maintain that because the records are universal, they therefore contain the history of other planets in the cosmos that are more technologically-advanced than Earth. The scientists of these older worlds will have progressed further in physics than their terrestrial counterparts and will doubtless have long accomplished telephonic communication and other technological advancements. Thus, all such achievements would be recorded in the Akashic repository.

How could the Akashic Records store such a phenomenal amount of universal data? No one seems able to answer that question but that doesn't mean that an explanation doesn't exist. After all, a laser hologram is a not dissimilar concept, yet this would have completely baffled scientists of the 1950s. We now know that if a photographic plate, containing the interference patterns of an object that has been recorded as a 3-dimensional hologram is shattered, the whole 3-D image can be recreated by shining a laser through one small sliver of the smashed plate. All the information about the total image of the object, has somehow been recorded onto every point of the plate. This discovery was not made until 1965 and was totally unexpected, so why should we dismiss the possibility of something similar on a far grander scale?

The Akashic Records are reputed to exist as a network of 'etheric space' which science has yet to discover. Perhaps through an altered state of consciousness of the kind experienced by Joe in his epileptic seizures, the Akashic databank can be accessed. We may know more one day.

The ghosts of Christmasses past

No book about ghostly goings-on would be complete without a selection box of Christmas hauntings. Ever since the debut of Jacob Marley in that literary classic, A Christmas Carol, by Charles Dickens in 1843, Yuletide has become a traditional time for the ghosts of the departed to visit their loved ones. What follows is a collection of eerie tales which took place during the season of goodwill; so settle into a fireside armchair and I will relate three strange stories about ghosts of Christmas past...

Daddy's Home for Christmas

The First World War was, without a doubt, one of the greatest upheavals in the history of the human race, involving 70 million combatants, 9 million of whom lost their lives. When this so-called Great War first broke out, in August 1914, millions of patriotic conscripts in Britain volunteered, rather lightheartedly, to go over to the trenches in France, believing that they would be making a victorious return home by Christmas of that year. In fact, the war dragged on for four long years and, during that eternity of horror, the soldiers were subjected to gas attacks, hand to hand combat and bayonet charges, constant barrages of high-explosive shells, snipers, typhus fever, rats, body lice, water-logged trenches and shell shock. Because of the strategic stalemate between the warring nations, the frontline soldiers, on both sides, spent most of their time confined to the trenches, cooped up with dismembered bodies and hideously-disfigured comrades.

In the first year of the war, on Christmas Eve, German and British soldiers alike pined to be at home with their families and friends. At midnight, snow began to fall and a strange hush descended on the cratered battlefields. Suddenly, the sounds of a distant choir drifted across no-man's land. It came from the German frontlines, less than 150 yards away, and it was a beautiful but saddening sound. They were singing Silent Night. Most of the soldiers caught up in the insanity of the conflict, suddenly realised that the unknown men they were fighting were not the ruthless, heartless demons the propagandists had painted them to be. The men on the other side of no-man's land longed to go home too. About an hour later, something very strange occurred on that freezing Christmas morning. Some of the Germans emerged from their trenches and walked unarmed to the middle of the neutral battlefied. One carried a leather football and he kicked it towards the startled British troops, who were surveying the courageous German soldiers with binoculars and periscopes. Three unarmed Tommies responded to the daring challenge. They emerged from a trench further down the line and went to meet their adversaries.

One of the men was a Liverpool-born man named George Wilkinson of the 1st Cheshire Regiment. He shook hands with one of the Germans, who offered him a cigarette. Wilkinson and his friends exchanged sweets and some cocoa for tobacco and tins of pressed beef, then sportingly kicked the football around. Soon, more troops from both fronts ventured into no-man's land. Some laughed and shook hands, while others openly wept and comforted one another with a hug or a pat on the back, even though they couldn't speak the same language. Many produced cherished photographs of their loved ones; of wives and babies, sons and daughters, mothers and fathers, who were spending Christmas back home without them. How they all longed to pack up and return to the life they knew. But the short cessation of hostilities didn't last long. Within the hour, the military commanders in Britain and Germany learned of the 'unpatriotic' meetings and wired an immediate order: the meetings between the opposing armies were to be terminated immediately, or heads would roll. And so, the soldiers from both sides shook hands and headed back to their trenches.

George Wilkinson thought about the strange encounter as he patrolled the trenches for the remainder of that morning. After his sentry duty, he lay down on the duckboards of his dugout and pulled a thick coat over himself. A knapsack over his tin hat was a makeshift pillow. As he started to fall asleep, his thoughts were with his family in Warrington. He could visualise his familiar little terraced home in the snow-covered street. Meanwhile, back in England, something very strange took place which has never been satisfactorily explained.

George's wife, Maggie, left her home and rushed across the street to her sister Joan's house. Joan was a reclusive widow and Maggie had invited her over for Christmas dinner but, typically, she hadn't turned up and she went over to find out why. While she was out of the house, her children, 6-year-old Jimmy and 5-year-old Lucy, were playing with their new toys in the parlour.

Jimmy was sitting on the hearthside rug in front of the coal fire, winding up his clockwork train, when he suddenly noticed a figure out of the corner of his eye. The boy turned and dropped the tin locomotive.

'Daddy!' he gasped. 'Daddy's home for Christmas!'

Lucy saw him too and her little round face lit up with joy. She and Jimmy charged at their father and he stooped down to pick them up. George had never been happier and he doubted his senses, unable to believe he was home at last. He hugged and squeezed his kids, then asked where their mother was.

'She's over at Aunty Joan's, Daddy.' Jimmy told him.

'Come on then, let's go and find her.' He took hold of his children's hands and they led him to the front door, out of the house and across the snow-covered street.

There was Maggie, standing on the other side of the road with Joan. The two women were gazing at the returned soldier in utter disbelief.

'Maggie!' George shouted then, suddenly, he wasn't there. His two children crossed the road alone. They were as baffled as Maggie and Joan and both were on the verge of tears as they looked around, trying to discover what had become of their father. Then Maggie noticed that only Jimmy and Lucy's footprints were visible in the snow.

A week after his solid-looking apparition had been seen by his children, wife and sister-in-law, George Wilkinson was killed by a German shell which left no trace of either him or his two companions.

In 1919, another soldier, Davey Harris, a friend of George, bumped into Maggie in Liverpool. He expressed his sorrow at Maggie's tragic loss and proceeded to tell her a strange story. A week before his death, George had told him about a strange and unusually lucid dream he'd had, in which he had visited his home and actually picked up his children and hugged them. George said he'd also seen his wife in the dream with her sister but, as he went to meet her, the bitter cold woke him up.

Maggie then told Davey about the apparition of her husband which had vanished as it came across the road towards her, on that Christmas day in 1914.

Until her death in 1964, Maggie Wilkinson held a personal vigil for her deceased husband every December, just in case he was able to make it home for Christmas.

The Christmas Gift

Amidst the rolling hills of Prestbury, in the late 19th century, there once stood an old cottage set in some hundred acres of land. This was the country retreat of a widowed Manchester magistrate, Samuel Gallimore. The judge spent the summer months in his secluded rural residence with his beautiful, 24-year-old twin daughters, Jane and Jennifer. There are strong links between most twins but Jane and Jennifer seemed to be both telepathic and empathetic. When they were seven, Jane fell from her horse and suffered concussion and, at the very moment of the riding accident, Jennifer, who was eight miles away from her sister at her uncle's house, suddenly fainted for no apparent reason. And, when Jennifer had her first passionate kiss from a boy at the tender age of nine, Jane blushed and felt her heart flutter, even though she wasn't anywhere near her sister at the time.

Jane and Jennifer were what is known as monozygotic twins. This means that they were conceived from one fertilised egg and shared identical sets of genes and were physically alike in every detail, even down to their fingerprints. The only tiny physical discrepancy that distinguished one from the other, was a very small mole on Jane's forehead, just above her left eyebrow. Of course, even identical twins can have quite different personalities and this was certainly so in this case. Jennifer was a vain megalomaniac who hogged the mirror, whereas Jane was a somewhat introverted and dreamy romantic.

One hot and humid day in June 1897, the twins left the cottage and wandered off for a picnic. They came upon an old gipsy woman named Peggy, who was picking borage flowers. Peggy had been pointed out to the twins before by their father, who had warned them not to talk to the Romany folk. However, the twins were burning with curiosity and disregarded their father's advice, for they had both read of the legendary powers of the gipsy people.

Jennifer asked Peggy if she had the power to look into the future of a person's life. The steely-eyed old woman simply nodded and, when Jennifer asked her to foretell her fortune, the gipsy held out her hand. Jennifer gave her a shilling and instantly old Peggy said,

'You'll woo many but never marry because you'll wait all your life, in vain, for your perfect man.'

'Nonsense!' Jennifer protested and demanded her money back but Jane told her to be quiet and asked the gipsy if she would reveal her future.

'You have no money,'

She was right, Jane had no money on her but she still pleaded to have her fortune told. Peggy suddenly turned and stared at her. For a moment she seemed to flinch, as if she had seen something dire in the girl's future.

'Oh dear!' was her only comment.

Jane followed Peggy and begged her to reveal what she had foreseen. The gipsy stopped in her tracks. She reached out and stroked Jane's long red hair and remarked enigmatically,

'Such fine hair. You'll never go grey, m'dear, and you will never lose your looks through age.'

'That doesn't make sense,' said Jennifer. 'she will age. Everyone grows old.'

Peggy pointed her finger at Jennifer and said,

'Aye, you will, but Jane won't.'

As the gipsy woman walked off, Jane called after her,

'How did you know my name?'

But no answer came back.

Three weeks later, the twins fell under the spell of a local amateur painter named Adam Kinglsey, who had set up his easel on nearby

Hare Hill. With his Van Dyck beard and golden, sun-bleached, shoulder-length hair, Adam looked just like the archetypal struggling artist. He dipped his sable brush in his pallette and attempted to capture the likeness of the landscape with a series of dramatic, jerky strokes across the wide canvas. The result was a mishmash of smears, which bore only a childish resemblance to the country scene. But the girls didn't regard Adam, who was a carpenter by trade, as some dabbling artistic dilettante; they were infatuated with him and were soon competing for his affections. It quickly became clear that Jane was his choice even though he only recognized her by the minute mole on her forehead, because the twins always dressed identically and wore their long hair in the same fashion.

Jennifer was naturally heartbroken; not soley because of her unrequited love for Adam, but because he was rapidly becoming a wedge between her and Jane. He seemed to have an almost hypnotic hold over her sister and his mask of gentleness soon slipped to reveal a dominating bully, who continually picked away at Jane's fragile self-esteem.

The twins' father was not at all keen on the artistic carpenter and he pleaded with Jane to end the courtship immediately but she was besotted with Adam. One night, Jane didn't return home and Jennifer knew instinctively that her sister had slept with the artist.

In August, Judge Gallimore was ready to return to Manchester but Jane could not be found. Then a letter arrived, telling her father and sister that she had gone to Paris with Adam, where she would soon be married to him. Judge Gallimore was furious, but there was little he could do, short of disowning his wayward daughter.

In 1898, Adam Kingsley's paintings were exhibited at Vollard's gallery, which was little more than a glorified shop on the Rue Laffite in Paris but the exhibition was a disaster. Not a single painting was sold and Jane had to support them both by working in a cafe. Kingsley continued to paint in a rented hovel of a garret on the left bank of Paris but still no one would buy his work. The disillusioned carpenter finally burned all his canvasses in a fit of rage and then revealed that he had been seeing a French girl. Adam further devastated Jane by telling her that he no longer loved her and ordered her to get out of his life. He ignored all her pleading and screamed that it was over.

Jane walked out of the apartment sobbing uncontrollably and, on the following morning, her body was fished out of the Seine. During those last, desperate minutes, as Jane drowned in the river, her sister Jennifer was at a dance in Cheshire. She struggled for breath and the colour drained from her face. She seemed to be choking and fought through the dancing couples to get out of the hall and into the fresh air. When she had finally regained her breath, she became visibly distressed, because she knew that something dreadful had just happened to her sister.

In 1950, at the age of eighty-five, the spinster, Jennifer Gallimore received a Christmas present from a Liverpudlian friend. When she unwrapped the gift, she almost fainted with shock. It was a white plaster plaque displaying the face of a woman with her eyes closed. The face wore a strange grin but was startlingly familiar. In fact, she soon recognised it as her own, or was it Jane's? Because the little mole over the left eyebrow was evident, Jennifer made enquiries about the plaque's origin and learned that it had been purchased in Lewis's. She visited the department store and asked the manager where it had been manufactured and found that it had been one of fifty imported from France.

She obtained the address of the French firm and wrote to them, asking if they had been made from an original mould of a model's face. The manager confessed that he did not know but promised to find out and, months later, he sent Jennifer the results of his investigation. He had discovered that the original mould for the plaques had been made from the face of an unknown girl who had committed suicide in Paris in the late 1890s. The original had been inscribed with the title 'L'Inconnue' – which means 'the unknown'. He then explained that, after the girl had drowned in the Seine, her body had been dragged from the river and displayed on a slab in the Paris Morgue, in the hope that someone would identify her and claim the body. No one came forward but, even in death, 'L'Inconnue' looked so hauntingly beautiful and serene, that artists flocked to sketch her and she developed something of a cult following.

Before decomposition destroyed her youthful, porcelain complexion forever, one artist was granted permission to cast a death mask of her face. Three days afterwards, the corpse was given a pauper's burial. Over the years, the mask was lost, then rediscovered and subsequently mistaken as a work of art. Mould-makers who were unaware of the original plaque's dark and tragic history, had subsequently used it to produce hundreds of ornamental wall tablets.

The old woman broke down and wept when she realised she was holding the death mask of her twin sister. Her wrinkled hands stroked the contours of the face and she sighed as she realised, with a chill, that the seemingly nonsensical prediction of the old gipsy woman, Peggy, had come to pass. Jane hadn't lived long enough for her hair to turn grey and her looks, frozen forever in the death mask, had cheated the ravages of time.

The Last Christmas Alone

The following bizarre story began to unfold at Neston on the Christmas Eve of 1990.

About a week before Christmas, Carl, a 43-year-old bachelor, lost his mother to cancer. He had been caring for her night and day, fervently hoping she would make it to Christmas, but it just wasn't to be. As Carl was decorating the Christmas tree for his mother, she suddenly said,

'You're a good son, Carl,' and passed away in her armchair.

Carl cried like a baby when he realised his mother had died and, when Christmas Eve came, he took down all the decorations and threw the Christmas tree into the loft, along with the gift-wrapped presents he'd bought for his mother. He felt so angry, losing his mother at a time of the year when families were supposed to be together. He had no one now. His father had died five years before from a heart attack and his only sister lived in Canada and she never phoned him or even sent him a card. Having devoted all the past few years to looking after his mother, he had lacked the opportunity to find a girlfriend and now, at the age of forty-three, he feared he would be permanently left on the shelf.

So, on this Christmas Eve, Carl sat in his bedroom swigging whiskey from a bottle, wallowing in self-pity. He looked out of the window and could see families visiting their relatives and friends. Then he noticed an old friend, Bob, whom he hadn't seen for years, walking down the other side of the street. Carl was about to open the window and shout to him when he saw him stop in front of the house opposite. He knocked on the door and, almost instantly, a beautiful blonde girl came out and hugged him. Together, they walked hand in hand down the street, laughing and kissing.

Carl's heart sank. This little scene had underlined his loneliness. He sat on the end of his bed and wondered if it was worth going on.

'What's the use, eh?' he sighed, as he wistfully remembered the Christmasses he'd spent with his parents when he was young. He reminisced about those golden years surrounded by a loving family and friends and even his loyal old dog, Jack. In those happy days, Carl never dreamt he would end up alone, with no one to love and no one to love him. He became choked with sorrow as he went over and over these nostalgic, childhood scenes.

What really topped that sad Christmas Eve was the poignant Christmas Card he found addressed to him from his late mother. She had secretly written the card and left it in the letter rack on the mantlepiece. She had evidently known she wouldn't be able to celebrate Christmas with her devoted son and, in the card, she wrote:

'I'd better wish you a Merry Christmas now, Carl. I love you, son, and I'm so grateful you looked after me. When I'm gone, please don't be bitter and settle down with someone who will love you.'

Carl bowed his head and cried.

'Merry Christmas, Mum, wherever you are.'

As he wiped the stinging tears from his eyes, he heard voices downstairs, apparently singing carols. He had had enough and he decided to confront the singers and tell them to get lost, because he had nothing to celebrate.

He stormed out of the bedroom clutching his bottle of whiskey, intending to give the carol singers an unseasonal earful but, as he reached the bottom of the stairs, his heart jumped, when he realised that theys were not outside in the street at all but in his front parlour.

Carl surmised that a crowd of drunken intruders had somehow broken into the parlour and he cautiously peeped in. A couple of strangers were sitting on the stool in front of the old stand-up piano, with their backs to him. A dark-haired man was playing a rendition of the old Bing Crosby classic, White Christmas, and a woman with long, red hair sat alongside him, with her head on his shoulder and her left arm curled around his waist. Stranger still, a small girl around six years of age, also with long, red hair stood to the left of the piano, gazing at the couple with a beautiful dreamy smile on her face. To their right, stood a small black boy, around the same age as the little girl. He wore a paper party hat and held a red balloon and seemed equally entranced by the music. Perched on top of the piano was a black cat. Its tail writhed warily to and fro as it caught sight of Carl peeping round the door. Suddenly, the little girl turned and also caught sight of Carl. Her mouth dropped open with shock, then she pointed to Carl and called out,

'Daddy! Look!'

A split second later, the parlour was in darkness and there was nobody there, just the old piano with its keyboard cover locked.

Carl realised he had just witnessed a family of ghosts and he fled into the street in fright. He was certain that he had not seen some alcohol-induced illusion. In fact, the ghostly encounter had sobered him up and had helped to take his mind off his bereavement and he managed to get through Christmas and the New Year without further tears.

In February of the following year, Carl mustered up enough courage to ask out a local librarian, called Nicola. She found him to be the most romantic man she had ever dated and soon fell head over heels in love with him. However, one day she started to cry and confessed that she had been keeping a secret from him. He persuaded her to trust in him and learnt that she had a one-year-old baby girl from a previous relationship. The father had deserted her while she was pregnant, after declaring that he could never settle down to bring up a family. The baby, Stacey, was being looked after by Nicola's mother. Carl told her that it didn't affect his feelings for her and he accepted responsibility for Stacey and doted on her as if she was his own child.

The couple settled down in Carl's house and they later adopted a 5-year-old black child, Danny. By the Christmas of 1996, Nicola discovered she was pregnant with Carl's child and, on Christmas Eve, the family assembled in the parlour. They played games like any other family and, before the children were put to bed for the most exciting night of the year, Carl and Nicola sat on the stool in front of the old piano and embraced. Then he played an old Christmas favourite of his mother's; Irving Berlin's, White Christmas. They all laughed when the family's black cat, Midnight, jumped onto the keys, then climbed onto the top of the piano. As Carl played the notes of the song, a tear trickled from his eye, as he pictured his old, sick mother sitting in her armchair, putting on a brave face and pretending she wasn't in pain. Nicola put her arm around him and gave him a reassuring hug, as little Danny looked on with his paper party hat, fidgeting with a red balloon. Suddenly, the fur on the cat's back bristled and Stacey called out,

'Daddy! Look!'

She pointed at something in the hallway. When the others looked to see what she was pointing at, they saw nothing.

'It was a ghost, Daddy!' Stacey exclaimed and she grabbed her mother's hand and told her, 'he had a sad face, Mummy.'

Carl went into the hallway to confirm that it was empty. He knew by his daughter's shocked demeanour that she wasn't playing a prank. Then an amazing realisation finally dawned on him. He cast his mind back four years to that lonely Christmas Eve when he had looked into the scene. He recalled the couple at the piano and how the woman had long, red hair, just like Nicola and how the man had been playing White Christmas, just as he had a minute ago. He also recollected seeing Danny in his party hat and the little girl with red hair who had spotted him peeking around the doorway.

He then accepted that what he had seen that sad Christmas Eve was a preview of his own future, happy, family life. So little Stacey had not seen the ghost of a dead person lurking in the hallway, but the spectre from a lonely Christmas past.

Don't fear the Reaper

Dressed in a monk's garb and carrying a scythe, the shadowy figure of the Grim Reaper is said to appear at the bedside of those who are about to leave this world. This personification of impending death is surely just a laughable relic from medieval times? Surprisingly, a number of well-respected paranormal investigators, studying near-death encounters, have noted the frequent reports of sinister figures which appear to the dying, apparently ready to escort them to the hereafter. American, Mark Chorvinsky, one of the world's leading paranormal researchers, has investigated more than a hundred sightings of reaper-like entities over recent decades. Chorvinsky says many of the reports of these eerie, supernatural ushers describe the Grim Reaper as a gentle and patient counsellor, who helps people through death or sometimes persuades them to stay alive. The physical descriptions of the Reaper vary from tall dark and handsome to the classic menacing image of a skeletal hooded figure carrying a scythe and hourglass. Chorvinsky claims,

'People I have interviewed are totally sincere. There are cases where there are mutiple witnesses, where two or more people who didn't even know the person who died, have seen the Grim Reaper.'

There have been numerous reports of the Reaper in Britain, including Cheshire. Here are just a few of these creepy accounts.

One evening in 1978 at a certain Cheshire hospital, a nurse froze in her tracks as she entered a darkened ward and spied a tall, hooded figure, dressed in monk's robes, standing by an old lady's bed. The nurse, Jean, reported that,

'His face was hideous. Just a skull with tiny flickering flames for eyes. His skeletal hands were folded over each other, inside his dark sleeves. I got the impression that the apparition was patiently waiting for the old lady to pass away. When it looked at me, my blood ran cold and I felt paralysed for a moment. The next thing I knew, I was running down the corridor to summon the other nurses. When we returned, the figure had gone and the old lady he'd been watching had passed away.'

In 1991, a businessman and his wife were staying at a hotel in Chester. At around 11pm, Monty went into the bedroom and was shocked to see a figure standing there in a long, black, hooded robe. The face of this apparition was a gleaming white skull with black eye sockets. In one of its bony hands it held a long scythe. He felt so faint with shock and his legs were so weak, that he was unable to run from the room. The figure glided towards him and announced in a low, bloodcurdling voice,

'Your wife wants to end her life. You must stop her.'

As Monty pondered the message, the figure vanished. His wife was was only in the bathroom, so he knocked on the door and heard her sobbing. He barged in and found her sitting on the rim of the bath, clutching a bottle of sleeping tablets. She had been contemplating suicide after finding several lumps in her breast. Monty later convinced her to go along to the hospital, where the lumps were found to be benign.

In 1995, Mike, a soldier with the territorial army, was camping in the woods at Swan Green near Lower Peover. The time was 4am and he was on sentry duty, wrapped in his cagoule, sitting in the small rounded hollow of a tree's gnarled roots. The other soldiers were dotted about the woods in their tents sleeping soundly and the only light came from the waning moon suspended above the horizon. Mike suddenly noticed a tall, dark silhouette silently approaching in the faint moonlight. He clicked on his powerful MagLite torch and directed its beam at the stranger. What that torch revealed has haunted Mike ever since. The figure was abnormally tall – almost seven feet in height – and dressed in a black, one-piece, hooded garment which trailed down to the ground. The ghastly pale face, with dark circles about the eyes, was not skeletal.

Mike was unarmed and felt defenceless against the freakish-looking prowler. He was about to shout to his sleeping comrades when he saw one of the soldiers leave his tent to confront the giant. He recognised the soldier as Barry, who was renowned as something of a daredevil in the TA squad. Mike jumped up, ready to support his mate but, when he got to his feet, the menacing, lanky figure was nowhere to be seen and nor was Barry. He woke up the squad and was surprised to find Barry in his campbed. At this point, Mike thought he'd dreamed the whole weird incident, until a soldier tried to wake Barry and got no response. He seemed to be in a comatose condition and, fifteen minutes later, a medic pronounced him dead. He'd apparently died of natural causes without regaining consciousness.

With a shudder, Mike recalled the mysterious tall figure who had visited the camp and left with what must have been Barry's shade.

Animals and the paranormal

Mohandas Gandhi once said that, 'The greatness of a nation and its moral progress can be judged by the way its animals are treated.'

The British have long been regarded as a nation of animal lovers but, even in ancient times, many other cultures venerated cats and dogs, especially the Egyptians, who domesticated the dog about 7500 BC. Of course, long before that, in the Stone Age, the dog was a human companion, acting as a friend, guardian, hunter and herder. The nocturnal cat, on the other hand, has always been regarded as a sinister creature, because of its very secretive and selfish nature. In medieval times, it was thought that Satan's favourite form was a black cat and spinsters having such a pet were usually accused of being witches. In ancient Rome, the cat was a symbol of liberty because no other animal is so carefree and unrestrained.

There is still a widely-held but prejudiced belief that animals have no souls, because they are somehow beneath man. To many humans, animals are savage brutes without intelligence or morals, but I disagree with that simplified and bigoted view. As the writer, Mary Ann Cross, once wrote,

'Animals are such agreeable friends; they ask no questions, they pass no criticisms.'

Another writer who held animals in high esteem, was the American poet Walt Whitman, who declared,

'I think I could turn and live with animals, they're so placid and self-contained... they do not sweat and whine about their condition, they do not lie awake in the dark and weep for their sins... not one is demented with the mania of owning things.'

Nevertheless, how often do we brand murderers and vicious criminals as 'animals'? Animals only kill out of necessity; for food, or to protect themselves and their young. The concept of the soulless animal undoubtedly stems from the arrogant belief that all creatures below man – including the embarrassingly human-like primates – are pea-brained dullards. In the 1970s, a neurophysiologist, John Lilly, was studying dolphin behaviour at the Marine World Aqua Zoo in Redwood City, California. Dr Lilly was recording the complex, warbling sounds of the dolphins with underwater microphones, when he and his fellow researchers heard something which was to cause a furore among behaviourists and marine biologists alike. A particularly extroverted bottle-nosed dolphin apparently uttered the sentence,

'Throw me the ball.'

The sentence was spoken in Hungarian and that particular dolphin had been a calf in a Budapest aquarium. The talking dolphin was taped uttering many other sentences but Dr Lilly's claims were not even investigated. Whatever the truth of the matter, it is a scientific fact that the brain of a dolphin has a highly-developed structure, which is more complex than the brain of an ape. Many respected biologists and neurologists even claim that the brain of the dolphin is superior to the human brain. The dolphin's neocortex – or thinking part of the brain – is larger and more convoluted than the neocortex of the average human. The high degree of development of the cortex in dolphins, suggests that the faculties of philosophical speculation, problem solving and even humour, may be present in these friendly sea creatures.

Some land mammals may also have more intelligence than we credit them with. A case in point is the cunning fox which was constantly hunted by a farmer at Lower Peover in 1796. One day, while the farmer was out with his dogs, stalking the fox, the hunted animal, seeing that the door of the farmhouse had been carelessly left ajar, nipped into the building and startled the farmer's wife, who was terrified of foxes. The fox seized one of the farmer's shirts in its mouth and pulled it over to the fire, until the garment was alight. The farmer's wife screamed and fled from the building, as the fox ran amok in the room, shaking the flaming shirt. The curtains caught fire and so did the cross beams of the dwelling. The bushy-tailed arsonist then fled and, despite the brave efforts of the farmer's wife to extinguish the flames with pails of water, the farmhouse was razed to the ground!

There are also many, well-documented stories of intelligent horses. In Elizabethan England, a bay gelding, called Morocco, had quite a repertoire. When a silver coin was presented to the horse, it would indicate how many pence were equivalent to it. The animal became so famous, it even earned a mention in Shakespeare's, 'Love's Labour Lost'.

If we accept that animals may be more intelligent than we assume, can we be so wholeheartedly sure that they do not possess some spark of spiritual essence akin to the human soul? How else can we explain the following reports of ghostly animals?

Since the 1870s, a phantom wild white stallion, known as the White Devil, has haunted the American prairies but Cheshire, too, has its phantom horses. For over a century, a white horse has been seen in broad daylight galloping through fields running parallel to the A54, between Allgreave and Danebridge. The spectral steed has been spotted by scores of motorists over the years, but the animal always fades away on the approach to the village of Wincle. It may be the apparition of a 17th century horse that bolted from a stable and went on the rampage until it was shot near Wincle.

Another ethereal horse haunts the grounds of Higher Huxley Hall, at Chester. However, this four-legged phantasm is not riderless but mounted by a phantom horseman. Some think the apparition is of a tenant farmer, John Salmon, who hanged himself from a beam in one of the Hall's farm buildings in 1810. The reason for Salmon's suicide has been lost with the passage of time but there were rumours that he was a sinister, second-sighted man and the appearances commenced soon after this suicide. Incidentally, the beam from which he hanged himself is still visible in one of the outbuildings of the hall and is carved with his name.

Cheshire's most famous ghost horse is said to be the Marbury Dunne. It is doubtful whether the ghost of this 18th century mare still gallops through the ancient parish of Great Budworth but here's the tale behind this Cheshire legend.

Lord Barrymore of Marbury Hall, Great Budworth, was a handsome and popular young man who had one consuming vice; he was an inveterate gambler and spent most of his youth in the private gambling clubs of the capital. Many women tried without success to tame the young, aristocratic gambler but, one day, a particularly charismatic and beautiful young lady was introduced to him and within days he had proposed to her. Lord Barrymore loved his bride-to-be so much, he promised that she could have anything her heart desired as a wedding gift. The lady chose a fine, greyish-brown, thoroughbred known as the Dunne Mare, which had caught her eye.

Lord Barrymore made a solemn promise that the horse would arrive in time for their wedding at Marbury Hall. While his future wife journeyed back up to Cheshire to prepare for the spectacular wedding, Barrymore remained in London to savour his last few days as a bachelor. During an all-night card party, the free-flowing wine went to his head and he bet that the Dunne Mare could leave London at sunrise and arrive at Marbury in time to greet the wedding guests by sunset. The seven other gamblers thought that Barrymore was mad but gladly accepted the wager. And so, on the wedding morning, up went a tremendous cheer from a crowd of Londoners as the horse bolted off into the northern suburbs of the capital, wearing specially made silver shoes and ridden by an amateur jockey. In Cheshire, the wedding took place and, later that day, as the sun turned red and was sinking behind the hills of Great Budworth, Lord Barrymore's sceptical friends laughed and waited eagerly to collect their winnings.

Then a young man with opera glasses pointed excitedly to the horizon, where a cloud of dust had appeared,

'It's the Dunne Mare! She made it!' he announced as he passed the glasses to Lord Barrymore.

The silver-shoed mare came thundering towards the astounded wedding guests. Lord Barrymore's new wife started to cry with joy at the sight of her magnificent wedding gift, advancing in a blaze of sunset-tinted dust.

The horse reached its destination and seemed very unsteady after the 200 mile, Olympian journey. As the steaming, sweat-drenched animal was led towards a well to be doused with fresh cold water, its legs collapsed and it belly-flopped to the ground. The poor Dunne Mare whined, as its parched tongue flopped out of its muzzle. Its eyes rolled and it struggled to get up but the effort proved too much and the exhausted creature keeled over and died. Lady Barrymore let out a dreadful scream and ran over to the dead animal. She felt its chest but could detect no heartbeat. The steam was still rising from its body but there was nothing anybody could do to resuscitate the horse. The animal was later laid to rest in a special grave near the well, in the grounds of Marbury Hall and the headstone bore the following inscription:

Here lie the bones of the Marbury Dunne,

The finest Mare that ever run,

Clothed in a linen sheet,

With silver hooves upon her feet.

Barrymore's wife took the death of her beloved horse very badly and refused to eat for over a week. She became so weakened by her fast, that she contracted a mysterious disease and fell seriously ill. She made a dying request to her husband; she asked to be buried next to the horse she had loved so dearly. Lord Barrymore promised to fulfil her wish but, after her death, he had her buried in the churchyard, as he feared the public outrage that would ensue, if his lady was interred near the well.

Three days after the funeral, Lord Barrymore and several servants were returning to the Hall one evening, when they were terrorized by an apparition of Lady Barrymore, charging at them on the shade of the Dunne Mare. It is alleged that the ghost of the Marbury Dunne is still occasionally seen cantering about the grounds, after dusk.

In 1994, the ghosts of two dogs apparently saved a young student's life. This strange incident took place in the Windmill Hill area of northern Cheshire. A young student, Chelsea, went to stay with her aunt in Southwood Avenue for the weekend. While Chelsea's aunt popped out to the shops, she stayed in to watch the television and began to feel drowsy. She was nearly asleep, when she was woken by the yapping of a frantic jack russel and the barking of a podgy black labrador. For some reason, she found it hard to get off the sofa and was having difficulty breathing. She started to doze off again but the dogs barked and whined to rouse her. She managed to get to her feet, then staggered to the door and opened it. She stumbled into the hallway and collapsed.

When Chelsea regained consciousness, her anxious-looking aunt was kneeling beside her, waiting for an ambulance to arrive. She was subsequently treated for carbon monoxide poisoning caused by a blockage in the gas fire's flue. Chelsea later said that it was lucky her aunt's dogs had alerted her but her aunt was puzzled as she had never kept a dog. A week afterwards, a neighbour mentioned that two dogs, a Jack Russel and a black Labrador, had lived in the house twenty years back. Since that weird occurrence, Chelsea's aunt has frequently heard the patter of paws in the hall, especially at night.

Mankind acknowledges only five senses, yet animals have many more senses at their disposal. Consider the sea salmon which can unerringly find its way back to the stream in which it was hatched, many miles distant. Some salmon swim from Alaska to Korea, using the sun and a heightened sense of smell as a compass. Just how they locate a particular stream remains a mystery. Equally mysterious, is the Arctic tern, which migrates over 16,000 miles from its Arctic breeding grounds in the far north of Siberia, North America and Europe, to the shores of Antarctica. The bird flies 24 hours a day on its pole-to-pole journey, for eight months, without any navigational aids. The tern and salmon are just two examples of creatures using poorly-understood sensory abilities. Pigeons, robins and seagulls are known to be able to detect tiny changes in the Earth's magnetic field and many other birds can recognize the patterns of star constellations, perhaps to orientate themselves on migratory journeys. Experimental evidence has also proved that cats, dogs and horses have a built-in direction finder, which enables them to find their way home over vast distances. This homing instinct is still an enigma. The super-senses of animals have also been employed in some countries as early-warning alarms for earthquakes, avalanches and other natural disasters.

Stories of animals detecting visitors from the supernatural realm have been reported for centuries. One rainy January evening in 1979, Alistair MacPherson, a librarian, settled down in the parlour of his Helsby home, to read a book in front of a blazing fire. Curled up on the fireside rug, was his tabby cat, Dunstan, seemingly fast asleep. Alistair was just getting into the second chapter of the book when Dunstan suddenly let out a hiss and arched his back. The cat stared squarely at his startled owner and bared his teeth.

'What's up with you, eh?' Alistair reached out to give his pet a reassuring stroke but the cat shrieked and shot behind an armchair. He surmised that Dunstan had experienced a nightmare of some sort but failed to coax it out of hiding for almost half an hour.

A week later, Alistair's cat gave a repeat performance. The time was just after 10pm and, once more, the librarian was reading his book when Dunstan shrieked and hissed at him without warning. On this occasion, the cat even raised its clawed paw towards its baffled and slightly bemused owner. At this moment, Alistair's friend, David, was approaching the house, to see if he wanted to join him down at the local pub for a drink. David went to the parlour window and lifted his hand to knock on the pane, when he saw something that shook him rigid. There was a sinister, gaunt-looking stranger, dressed in an outdated, long black coat, standing behind Alistair's chair, intently observing him. Alistair started when he saw David's shocked face peering in at him and, as he rose from his chair to admit him into the house, he momentarily obscured David's view of the creepy-looking man. When Alistair moved out of the way, the weird figure had vanished. David then noticed that his friend's cat was staring transfixed at the spot where the ghost had stood.

When David told Alistair about the apparition, his friend said that he had felt the hairs on the nape of his neck stand up several times that evening but had put it down to his imagination.

A fortnight later, Alistair was doing a crossword in the same, high-backed chair, when he suddenly sensed an icy presence behind him. Once again, the cat went berserk but this time Alistair got the fright of his life when he looked at his reflection in the window, because he could also see the reflection of a pale-faced man who was standing behind his chair, gazing at him intently. Now it became obvious why his cat had been acting so strangely. In one swift movement, Alistair bolted from his chair and raced out of the parlour straight to his friend's house, followed closely by his cat. That spooky encounter with the lurking apparition was the last straw and the librarian later moved out of the house. The identity of the curious ghost is unknown but, in 1910, a lodger had stabbed his landlord to death, in the parlour where the phantom was seen.

Spooky sounds and nocturnal noises

In the summer of 1977, people all over England suffered many sleepless nights due to a persistent humming sound of unknown origin. Complaints of an irritating, low-frequency hum had been reported in the south of England in the infernally-hot summer of 1976 but, in the following year, the almost infra-sonic drone suddenly spread northwards. It was described as sounding like a diesel or ship's engine, rising and falling in volume, often getting loud enough to irritate the eardrums. According to the 800 letters received from the tormented readers of The Sunday Mirror, the ubiquitous background hum was causing insomnia, deteriorating health, domestic friction and disturbed pet behaviour. One sufferer in Stockport was reduced to walking the streets at night, while a Manchester couple resorted to travelling around in their car for hours. A pensioner in Woolston went to her GP thinking she had tinnitus but her doctor said he too had heard the strange nocturnal sound and only got through the night by sleeping with the radio on! In Warrington and Liverpool people had their electricity meters changed and acoustic experts from the BBC tried to discover the direction of the mind-numbing din. They merely established that it was coming from every direction and no one could determine what was generating it.

The public and the experts variously blamed water pressure in pipes, North Sea oil-drilling, metal tooth-fillings picking up radio broadcasts, electric pylons and even UFOs. None of the theories, plausible or outlandish, fitted the facts. It was discovered that wearing earplugs or ear-muffs to escape the hum only made it worse. Sometimes, the hum was localized in one particular area of a dwelling. A farmer near Farndon, on the Welsh border, was intrigued by the way the low whirring sound could only be heard in one corner of a barn. He called in an electrician to check if the sound was from a mains wire that ran past the barn but, even when the mains supply was switched off, the hum persisted.

An MP pleaded for the Government to carry out investigations but his request was flatly turned down on financial grounds. The head of acoustics at Liverpool University also applied to the Science Research Council for a grant to solve the mystery but his application was refused too and, by the end of the 1970s, the hum had faded away. Similar inexplicable, low-pitched noises are occasionally still heard in England and many other parts of the world, including Antarctica, but the phenomenon remains an enigma.

Much less subtle than the hum, but just as mystifying, are the phantom sonic booms heard over western Cheshire and Clwyd. Over several nights towards the end of January 1974, scores of people in Cheshire reported seeing strange coloured lights whizzing silently across the sky in a V-shaped formation. Ironically, these UFOs were even spotted in the skies over Jodrell Bank, where the enormous radio telescope scans deep space for evidence of extraterrestrial life. The Liverpool Echo and several local newspapers in Cheshire and Wales gave the UFO sightings several column inches and experts cited the usual debunking explanations, as a rebuff to the UFO interpretation. People had obviously mistaken the planet Venus (which doesn't fly in formation), or city lights shining on migrating birds (in January?). The story of the lights in the sky was about to pass into obscurity, when something happened which is still the subject of much controversy today.

At 8.38pm on 23rd January of that year, a powerful earth tremor, which measured 4.5 on the Richter Scale, was recorded by the Global Seismology Unit at the Institute of Geological Science in Edinburgh. The tremor also shook the recording pen of a seismograph at Greenwhich. The only puzzle was that the tremor did not exhibit the familiar characteristic curve of a normal quake; the shape traced by the recording pen suggested that something akin to a meteorite had slammed into Britain with a tremedous force. The epicentre of the 'skyquake' was soon determined; it was somewhere in the Berwyn Mountains, near Llandrillo, in Clwyd. Seconds before the Welsh mountains shook, people in Western Cheshire and parts of North Wales, saw a blue-green streak of light crossing the sky, so it was naturally assumed that a meteorite had fallen on Wales. However, a subsequent thorough search of the Berwyn Mountains failed to discover any evidence of a crater or even the slightest trace of a meteorite. Yet, the blast had been powerful enough to generate a sonic boom which shattered windows in Southport, cracked two mirrors in Liverpool and set off burglar alarms in factories at Ellesmere Port. The loud bang and ground judder was reported as far away as Preston, Blackpool, Manchester, Stoke-on-Trent and Shrewsbury. There were claims from locals in Clwyd that an enormous spacecraft had smashed into the Berwyn Mountains, scattering debris and alien bodies for miles. Rumours also circulated of a massive military cover-up but no trace of the purported UFO wreckage was ever produced to back up the incredible claims.

Two years after the mysterious Berwyn explosion, a second sonic boom and simultaneous tremor rocked the North West of England, on the night of 6th August 1976. This second seismic shockwave was felt over a ten mile radius and, once again, something in or above the Berwyn Mountains was the source of the powerful earth-shaking blast. This time, the skies over Wales, Cheshire, Merseyside and Southern Lancashire lit up during the blast and remained luminous for several minutes. An ex-military scientist wrote to his local MP, suggesting that IRA terrorists had conducted an underground nuclear testing of a home-made atom bomb. Once again, police and Ministry of Defence officials combed the Berwyn Mountains for clues but nothing was found. To this day, no one knows what rocked North West England twice during the 1970s.

The final sonic mystery of this chapter is nowhere near the decibel magnitude of the Berwyn booms but it is just as thought-provoking. It all began in Daresbury, the Cheshire village where Lewis Carroll was born, in 1832. For over a week, in the autumn of 1970, several villagers were roused from their sleep at 4.30am by the relentless blast of a distant car horn. Each time the horn was heard, the police and several angry residents, would embark on a fruitless search for what they predicted to be some insomniac, with a liking for practical jokes. On each occasion, the deafening sound would stop dead, at precisely 4.37am.

After a week of cherished silence, the mysterious horn pierced the still night air again at 4.30 in the morning. This time, two policemen managed to home in on the source of the noise pollution and what they came across sent a shiver up their spines. A mini car had skidded off a road and impacted into the trunk of a huge oak, on the northern outskirts of the village. Inside the crumpled vehicle, the long-haired driver, a 23year-old student from Blackburn, was dead from the terrible injuries he'd sustained. The steering wheel was embedded in his chest. At precisely 4.37am, the mini's horn stopped abruptly. This naturally made the policemen and several Daresbury residents, speculate about the horn they had heard a week earlier. Had it been some sort of portent of the fatal car crash?

Not a blade of grass

In the late summer of 1821, a widow in the Welsh town of Montgomery, wrote to a young Cheshire man, John Davies, with whom she had become acquainted many years before, asking him if he would help her on her run-down farm. Davies wrote back saying it would be a pleasure to help her but, as soon as he arrived in the town, the clannish community seemed to resent his presence and backs were turned upon both him and the widow.

One afternoon in September, Davies was on an errand for the widow when he was attacked by Welsh highwaymen, who demanded his money. He refused and fought the two men but was badly beaten. Then, to add insult to injury, the two local thugs claimed that Davies had attacked them and accused him of being their attacker. They then took their victim to Welshpool, where he was charged with highway robbery. The two genuine robbers testified, in what was little more than a kangaroo court and Davies was found guilty and sentenced to death. The young man loudly protested his innocence but those present just ignored him and chatted amongst themselves in Welsh. Within hours, Davies was on the scaffold and the hangman was binding him up.

Before his arms were tied, he lifted his right hand and declared,

'I die, praying to God that he will let no grass grow on my grave, to prove my innocence!'

The hangman pulled Davies' arm down and tied it tightly to his other hand, then impatiently pulled the lever without even placing a hood over the young man's head. He fell through the trap-door to his mercifully-swift death. As his body swung, lifeless, on the creaking rope, there was a deathly hush in the crowd, as they all reflected upon the hanged man's last words.

The widow was naturally devastated and she had her friend buried in Montgomery parish churchyard. A band of the ghouls who had turned out for the hanging, loitered at the gates of the churchyard, watching the sobbing widow lay flowers on the grave.

Months passed and people soon remarked how grass never grew over Davies' grave. All the other graves were covered with grass and had to be trimmed regularly but there was always a barren rectangle over Davies' resting place. A priest sprinkled the grave with grass seed but it failed to germinate. Thirty years afterwards, the cemetery was remodelled. New paths were laid and long strips of turf were placed over the graves but, within a fortnight, the grass over the grave of John Davies had withered and died, leaving a solid rectangle of infertile earth. A priest again placed squares of turf over the patch but this also shrivelled and died.

To this day, the grave of John Davies does not have a blade of grass upon it and this is recognised by locals as an everlasting sign of the lynched man's innocence.

Cheshire's witches and warlocks

Stratigraphy is one of the primary tools of archaeological interpretation and is based on the fact that where one deposited layer of earth overlies another, the upper layer must have accumulated later in time than the lower. This means that fossils can be dated from their surrounding strata. This geological record extends downwards from the ground you walk on, in chronological layers. If we dig down a few feet we may find coins from the Middle Ages but, if we continue to excavate, we could unearth the vestiges of a Roman camp; much deeper lie the fossilized remains of the dinosaurs. However, there are many 'anomalous fossils' which give the archaeologists and historians sleepless nights.

For example, in 1927 at Fisher Canyon, Nevada, a block of limestone was split open to reveal the fossilized imprint of a well-cut and double-stitched leather sole. The limestone block containing the shoeprint, was from the Triassic Era, which meant it was formed between 160 and 195 million years ago. Fossilized shoe-imprints have even been discovered in Carboniferous rock that was formed 300 million years before the advent of the dinosaurs. One such imprint, uncovered at Antelope Springs in Utah, showed a crushed trilobite, underneath a sandalled heel. A trilobite is an extinct marine creature which flourished 200 to 500 million years ago. In 1961, another anomalous fossil came to light when gem hunters in California X-rayed a 500,000-year-old nodule. The X-ray showed that the ancient rock contained something which looked identical to a modern sparking plug. The function of the cylindrical object and how it came to be encased in rock half a million years old, is still unanswered. Furthermore, in the Natural History Museum in London, the skull of a Neanderthal man is stored, which seems to have been blasted with a high-velocity bullet – over 40,000 years ago! On one side of the skull there is a small, perfectly-rounded hole and the damage to the other side of the skull is consistent with the effects of a high-velocity bullet being fired through the head. There have been many other incredible discoveries which, if accepted, could disprove the textbook version of prehistory and demolish the Darwinian theory of evolution.

The out-of-place fossils seem to back up the long-held claims of every culture; that in the remote past, there were many civilizations that reached the pinnacle of technological achievement before being wiped out by catastrophies. Our own civilization could share this fate tomorrow, through nuclear self-annihilation, or even from inter-planetary cataclysm.

At midnight, on Monday, 10th August 1998, the Earth came within six hours of being obliterated, as a giant, mile-wide asteroid hurtled past it, at over 50,000mph. The asteroid missed us by just under a million miles, which, on the cosmic scale, is quite a close shave. If the giant rock hadn't veered away from us, it would have killed over a quarter of the global population and created a gigantic tidal wave miles high. The asteroid was the largest in recorded history to have come so close to the Earth and the terrifying near-miss was only known to a select group of scientists, to avoid mass hysteria. It has been estimated that about once every 100,000 years, a comet or asteroid hits the Earth and once every century, a 50 metre object collides with us, causing an explosion 5,000 times that of the Hiroshima A-bomb. Some scientists even believe the dinosaurs were wiped out by an asteroid, which smashed into the Earth 65 million years ago.

The next known asteroid that will graze past the Earth, will be the 10 mile wide Toutatis, which will come within 13 hours of our world on 29th September 2004.

When we take the threat of catastrophe from space or the misuse of nuclear technology into consideration, it seems frighteningly plausible that perhaps there were civilizations in antediluvian times which reached their zenith only to be exterminated by a natural, or self-inflicted Armageddon. The occultists all over the world claim that magic, both black and white, is a fragmented remnant of super-science, used by the ancient masters millions of years ago. There are those who believe that some scientists from the lost golden age of man, survived the ancient disasters and upheavals and transmitted their cabalistic knowledge to various students down the ages. One quasi-historical personage who comes to mind, is the mysterious Merlin, the celebrated wizard who advised King Arthur.

The information on Merlin is very scant but it is recorded that he originated in Wales, possibly towards the close of the 5th century. Legend has it that Merlin was a powerful magician, who used levitation and other magical talents to construct Stonehenge. Some accounts say the Welsh wizard perished after a fierce battle between the Britons and their Romanized compatriots in the year AD 570, but other traditions maintain that he was trapped in a hollow rocky hill by Nimue, the enchantress. The whereabouts of this hill are unknown but a fable has persisted for centuries that names Cheshire's Alderley Edge as the site of Merlin's prison. Alderley Edge is a rocky sandstone escarpment which rises to over 600 feet above sea level and is over two miles long. This magnificent, brooding mound, with its breathtaking panoramic views over Macclesfield, gives the nearby town, a few miles south of Wilmslow, its name. Many visitors to the Edge have commented on the strong presence of a mysterious bygone age, which seeps into our dimension.

Excavations at Alderley Edge have established that ancient pagans mined the copper on its slopes and lit sacrificial bonfires on the summit. At the height of the witch-persecution mania in the 1640s, many covens who held regular sabbats at the Edge, had to disband and flee to Wales. Even today, witches and warlocks regularly congregate at the Edge, on certain nights of the year, to celebrate the old pagan gods of Ishtar, Pan, Diana and Samhain.

Early one morning in 1695, a farmer from Mobberley set off for Macclesfield market with a majestic, ivory-coated mare, which he intended to sell for a good price. To reach his destination, the farmer had to lead his horse across the lower slopes of Alderley Edge and it was here that something amazing took place. An old man, wearing a flowing black robe and a strange pointed cap, approached the farmer. The man held a staff and his beard was white as snow. He wished the farmer good day, then eyed the white mare and offered to buy it.

The farmer refused the offer saying he'd get a better price at Macclesfield market, but the old man confidently stated that the white horse would not be sold at the market and predicted that they would meet again, at the Edge, later in the evening. The farmer sneered and continued on his journey. However, much to his surprise, he was unable to sell his graceful horse at the market and, on his return journey to Mobberley, the old man once again appeared from nowhere in the same spot as before. This time he said nothing but motioned the farmer to follow him through the woods to the rock face. Intrigued, he trailed after the old man past a large rock called Stormy Point, where a strange sensation came over him, hypnotically impelling him to follow the stranger. The old man stopped and gazed at the blank sandstone face of Castle Rock, which forms the eastern side of the Edge. Wondering what would happen next, the farmer was mystified to see a kind of doorway open up in the rock face. The bearded man pointed his staff at the doorway, then walked through it. The farmer felt himself strongly drawn through the same doorway and found himself walking into an immense cavern, illuminated by a faint, amber phosphorescence. On the floor of the cavern, in one area, was an array of men in shining armour, lying side by side. They appeared to be sleeping and had shields and swords at their sides. In a sombre manner, the old man glanced at the sleeping warriors and explained that they were King Arthur and the Knights of Camelot, lying dormant in the chamber, until their country needed them.

It suddenly dawned on the farmer that the old man was Merlin, Arthur's mentor. But, before he could quiz him, he was given a heavy sack of gold coins, in exchange for the white mare and was ordered to leave the cave. He obeyed, glancing back just once more, to glimpse the sleeping knights and caught sight of the sorcerer laying down the now unconscious horse. Perhaps it too was being put into a state of suspended animation until such time as it would be revived to carry Arthur himself into a final great battle. As he left the hidden stronghold, the ground shook violently as the stone slab crashed down behind him.

Strangely enough, many visitors to Alderley Edge have reported seeing a rectangular shape in the face of Castle Rock which rapidly fades on close inspection. On returning to Mobberley and recounting his adventure, the farmer was greeted with ridicule. Yet no one ever put forward a satisfactory explanation as to where he had obtained his bag of gold coins, each of which bore the insignia of a dragon.

Today, a wishing well known as the Wizard's Well is to be found on the woodland path to Castle Rock, where the entrance to Merlin's cavern is said to be situated.

Just a couple of miles to the west of Alderley Edge, another supernatural incident allegedly took place in 1595. Ned Holden, a highwayman, was captured by the authorities and hanged. In the early hours of the morning, under a full moon, a vagrant named Gammin, on the road from Knutsford, spotted two figures cutting the hanged criminal down from the tree. He hid behind a hedgerow and watched as the two men carried the body into a nearby wood. Out of curiosity, Gammin decided to follow the body-snatchers, even though he was fearful of the consequences if the men saw him.

The men were John Gough and Toby Rodgers; two young dabblers in the Black Arts and avid students of the alchemist and mathematician, John Dee, who was, at that time, the warden of Manchester College. Gough and Rodgers had read Dee's books, which were branded as heretical and blasphemous.

The corpse was laid out in a clearing, beneath a lantern suspended from a branch. One of the men started to recite unintelligible words, while the other one knelt down by the corpse and scrutinised its face. Gammin looked on, fascinated, eager to discover what they were up to. He soon found out.

By the lantern's light, the corpse's mouth was seen to flicker. Then the eyelids opened wide to reveal two livid white eyeballs. Gammin felt faint as he witnessed the highwayman being re-animated by the black magic. He didn't know it, but Gough and Rodgers were practising the ancient and well-documented art of necromancy – raising a dead person back to life in order to obtain information.

One of the men was heard repeatedly asking the corpse where he had hidden the proceeds of his robberies. The highwayman's eyes rolled and, in a raspy, chilling voice, he asked,

'Where am I?'

The necromancer told him he was dead and damned to spend eternity in Hell unless he revealed the location of his treasure. The corpse made a moaning sound, then uttered a garbled reply about a well, situated by a dead-end lane. At this point, Gammin was spotted and chased by the black magicians but he managed to lose them in the woods. He alerted the authorities but Gough and Rodgers could not be found. The notorious pair were later sighted in Manchester but never caught. Gammin and scores of other people searched for the site of the well, in the hope of uncovering his hidden loot but it is not known if anything was ever found.

In the 1860s, an old Welsh hermit, Ivor Williams – who lived in a dilapidated cottage on the Cheshire border, near Worthenbury – was shunned by the locals, who believed him to be a wizard. In 1861, a man named McGowan was driving a wagon-load of wood across land adjacent to Williams' cottage when, for no apparent reason, the horses pulling the wagon stopped dead. McGowan soon discovered that it was not the horses, but the wagon, which was acting strangely. The wheels seemed to be locked tight. He then became aware of the elderly Mr Williams, standing in the doorway of his cottage, gazing intently at the wagon with his steely blue eyes. In the end, McGowan had no choice but to unhitch his horses, whereupon they instantly they trotted over to the hermit and stood motionless on his path, as he whispered something to them. Moments later, they galloped off. This naturally convinced McGowan of the truth of the rumours about Williams and he abandoned his timber-laden wagon and hurried on to Wrexham on foot.

In 1865, a number of superstitious farmers from Wales and Cheshire signed a petition to evict the sinister recluse on the grounds that he was a practising witch and, therefore, an anti-Christian. However, a local magistrate adjudicated that there was no evidence to support the claims that Williams was acting unlawfully in any way. In the summer of that year, the farmers who had tried to get rid of Williams claimed that he had caused havoc on their farms with his strange powers. Cattle fainted, mysterious fires broke out which razed farm buildings to the ground and, in July, something truly bizarre took place, one sunny afternoon, which even earned a mention in The Times newspaper.

Hundreds of people in Wrexham and parts of Cheshire were startled to see masses of hay drifting through the blue skies. Haymakers in Wrexham first noticed the strange spectacle but, as the flying hay moved in a north-eastwards direction (against the wind), more and more people saw the peculiar sight. Several witnesses came forward and claimed that they had seen a tonne of hay rise from the same farm outside Wrexham, which was owned by the initiator of the petition.

One night in 1869, Ivor Williams' cottage was gutted by a blaze but no trace of its curious and much-feared tenant was ever found in the smouldering ruins and his fate remains a mystery. The superstitious locals concluded that his disappearance after the blaze was simply a sign that Lucifer had reclaimed the old warlock.

The matchmaker

The curious tale which follows, concerning a mysterious matchmaker, took place in Haslington, near Crewe, in the mid 1980s and was even reported on a TV show called Phenomena.

In the autumn of 1985, Derek, a 39-year-old bachelor of Kidsgrove, near Stoke-on-Trent, lost his mother to cancer. He had been an only child and, as his father had died from a heart attack ten years earlier, he decided to move out of the rented, three-bedroomed house, which had been his home for the last twenty years. The place was now too big for him and held too many memories, so Derek looked around for a one-bedroomed flat. His cousin, Harry, had a friend who was letting a cosy, modern apartment in Haslington, seven miles from Kidsgrove. He viewed the flat and, finding it better than expected, paid a month's rent in advance. As a result of the move, he had to leave his job in Kidsgrove as a television repair man.

Derek soon settled into his new flat on the second floor of a renovated Edwardian house and spent most of the first week gazing at the pleasant view of the park. One morning, during that first week, he was looking out of his window, watching the leaves flutter down whilst contemplating the loss of his mother and the course of his own life, when he suddenly noticed a woman hurrying down the street. She was in her mid-thirties, with long black hair and a cherubic face. She wore a knee-length, royal blue coat and had a red scarf swathed around her neck. Despite her being over a hundred yards away, Derek thought her beautiful and found something graceful in the way she moved.

At the same time on the following day, Derek was waiting at the window, hoping he'd catch sight of the young woman again, when she came rushing down the street. For some reason, she glanced up at the window and looked at Derek. He smiled but she only responded by swiping back her sleeve to inspect her watch, before continuing on her way.

He decided to follow her, even though he realised he was becoming somewhat obsessed. Grabbing his coat and hurrying out, he looked down the street but could find no sign of her. He spent over an hour traipsing the neighbourhood in the vain hope of spotting her but the elusive woman was nowhere to be seen.

On the following day, which was a Sunday, Derek waited at the window from 8am till noon, but the woman haunting his thoughts failed to put in an appearance.

He was ready on Monday, however. He paced the length of the street running parallel to the park from 7.50am onwards and he spotted the object of his affections approaching him in a dark fur coat and a woollen hat. His heart leapt, as if he were a lovesick schoolboy. He bowed his head and pretended to study the leaf-strewn pavement to try and steady his nerves. When she was about twenty feet away, he raised his head and momentarily made eye contact. She had seemed older from the window but now, at close range, he could see that she was about twenty-five at the most and had a flawless, peaches and cream complexion. Her large, almond-shaped eyes swiftly looked him up and down before passing swiftly by.

Derek smiled with satisfaction and returned to his flat. He tried to concentrate on a television programme but his infatuation with the woman dominated his thoughts.

When she came down the street the following morning, Derek found himself trailing her like some crazy stalker, at a distance of about fifty yards. This time, he discovered that she was working in the local newsagents. After mustering all his courage, he entered the shop and bought a morning paper. He was disappointed when the man served him but, as he opened the till, he turned to the brunette and asked,

'How's your mother, Paula?'

Paula just sighed and replied,

'A lot better. Still got her cough though.'

Derek pocketed his change and left the newsagents, pleased that now he at least knew her name but, regretably, nothing else about her.

His second break came a few days later as he was walking along his pre-planned, morning route past the park. Paula came walking towards him and acknowledged him with a smile as she passed. Derek kept on walking but couldn't help glancing back at her. To his delight, he saw that she was looking back at him.

That evening, he paced his living room, aching to know where she lived. He hadn't dated a girl for seven long years and was absolutely clueless at approaching the opposite sex. He was just too introverted and self-conscious in such matters. Nevertheless, he thought that if he could find out her address, he could send her a letter explaining his feelings. It would be a faint-hearted thing to do but asking her out face to face would be just too daunting a prospect. He picked up a pen and writing paper and attempted to compose the letter but he just couldn't find the right words to express his feelings. Finally, he decided to drop the idea for the time being, consoling himself by arguing that these matters are better not rushed. Instead, he would pay a few more visits to the newsagents.

But Derek was in for an unpleasant surprise. When he next visited the newsagents, Paula was kissing her male colleague. He was so shocked that, when Paula looked towards him, startled at his presence, he turned and walked out without saying a word.

That night, something strange took place which has never been explained. After putting the milk bottles out, Paula bolted the front door and went upstairs to her bedroom. In the adjacent room, her flu-stricken mother was sound asleep. In another bedroom, down the landing, her 21-year-old brother was also asleep, while her father was in the living room, dozing in an armchair in front of the television.

At 1am, Paula's father woke up and switched off the television. As he entered the hall, he saw the outline of a woman through the frosted glass of the front door. She was wearing a headscarf tied in the 1950's style. As he looked on, the letterbox flap opened gently and an envelope dropped onto the mat. As he picked it up, he noticed that it was addressed to his daughter and quickly unbolted the door and yanked it open. He searched the street but found it empty in both directions. He woke Paula and showed her the mysterious envelope.

'Some woman put that through the door just now.'

Still half asleep, she took out the sheet of paper, unfolded it and scanned a poem at the top of the page which read:

Paradise would be,
A girl like you with me,
Under the moon and starry sky,
Like Romeo and Juliet,
A Piscean and a Gemini.

Paula blushed as she realised that the first letter of each line spelt out her name. Then she read the intimate, soul-baring narrative beneath the poem, written by someone who thought she was beautiful and longed to be her lover. The love-letter was simply signed 'Derek' and a post-script informed her that he would reveal himself the next morning at 8 o'clock, in the street near the park.

Paula re-read the last line of the acrostic poem and asked her bemused father,

'How does he know I'm a Piscean?'

'Oh, it's probably that fellah who works with you in the shop pulling your leg,'

But Paula knew that Keith, her workmate at the newsagents, was most definitely not one to have romantic thoughts and write love-letters; in fact, he wasn't that interested in Paula at all. On the day Derek had walked into the newsagents, he had only been messing about, showing Paula how his mate kissed girls.

At 8am the next day, Paula walked along the street adjacent to the park with a mounting sense of anxiety, wondering if Derek would show up at his rendezvous.

Derek meanwhile, was walking up the street towards his flat on the other side of the road. He'd been up all night, trying to come to terms with Paula being involved with someone else. He was returning from the filling station with a carton of milk, when he saw her approaching. His bruised heart sank and he crossed the road. She became suspicious, as she had noticed the way Derek had looked at her before. She recalled how he had immediately turned and left the newsagents when he had seen Keith kissing her. She knew it had to be him. He was the letter-writer. She stopped and shouted over to him,

'Oi!'

Derek stopped in his tracks near the entrance to his house and realised Paula was shouting to him. He was at a loss as usual as to how to respond and all he could manage by way of reply was,

'Eh?'

Paula blushed with embarrassment and crossed the road, trying to conceal her own shyness with a broad smile. She stood before him and coyly asked,

'Are you Derek?'

'Yeah, why?'

'Why did you write me that silly letter?'

Derek was obviously baffled.

'What letter? I don't know what you're talking about.'

'Oh you don't, do you?' said Paula, with a knowing look. 'Then why are you going all red?'

Derek was confused to say the least,

'Look, Paula, I swear I never wrote you any letter.'

'How do you know my name?' She thought she had caught the scribbling Romeo out.

'I've heard people calling you that name in the newsagents. I heard your boyfriend calling you Paula.'

'He's not my boyfriend,' Paula laughed, then added, 'My boyfriend works on an oil rig.'

Derek continued to deny any knowledge of the letter and stormed off to his flat but Paula was still convinced he was lying and went to work. The mysterious love-letter became a recurring topic of conversation throughout that week, whenever Derek visited the newsagents. And, a week later, Paula asked if he would like to take her out for a drink. He declined, saying he didn't want to antagonize her boyfriend when he returned from the oil rig. Upon which, Paula laughingly confessed that this boyfriend was just a figment of her imagination and so they finally went out on a date.

The couple were engaged for a year and later married. The real author of the love letter is still unknown. Whoever wrote it must have known their birth signs. That mysterious person who played Cupid also knew Paula's address and Derek's innermost feelings. It was as if it had been penned by some supernatural matchmaker.

The angel of twelfth night

Although the following strange tale happened in Liverpool, I have included it here because the main character was a Cheshire girl.

In the snowy December of 1962, a sixteen-year-old Runcorn girl, Rebecca Bramley, became totally infatuated with Eamonn Doherty, a young Liverpudlian. Eamonn had been staying at his cousin, Susan's, from Boxing Day to New Year's Eve and, during that time, he had become attracted to her best friend, Rebecca. Until she first set eyes on him in Susan's home, Rebecca had dismissed love at first sight as a silly romantic myth. But, from the first moment she and Eamonn had exchanged glances, she had become completely mesmerised by him.

On New Year's Eve, as the rest of Runcorn was preparing to celebrate the arrival of 1963, Rebecca was weeping in Susan's arms.

'Oh pack it in, Becky. Stop crying,' urged Susan, as she hugged her sobbing schoolmate.

'I love him. I want to go with him.' Rebecca had to force the words from her choked-up throat.

Meanwhile, downstairs, Eamonn was packing the couple of Christmas gifts from his aunt and uncle into his suitcase, ready to catch the train back to Liverpool. He wasn't too happy about leaving Rebecca but had promised to write and return in the summer, to take her on a visit to his city. The girl had really grown on him over the last week. It was as if he'd always known her.

Rebecca kept on pleading to go with him but he just shook his head and embraced the tearful girl. Then, suddenly, he had a change of heart and agreed to take her, with her parent's consent. When her parents both refused, her reaction was to put on her mother's fur coat and sneak out of the house. She assured Eamonn that her parents didn't mind her going and they were soon on the train, bound for Lime Street

Mr and Mrs Bramley were both furious and extremely anxious, when they learned what their daughter had done. They considered going to the police but approached Susan's parents instead and explained what had happened. The Bramley's were given Eamonn's address in a block of tenements called Lawrence Gardens, in the Scotland Road area of Liverpool. Mr Bramley wrote to his wilful daughter, imploring her to return home immediately and threatening to inform the police if she refused.

On New Year's Day, Eamonn took Rebecca to the landing stage at the Pier Head and bought her chips. They looked out over the choppy waters of the Mersey, discussing their future and making promises. Rebecca asked Eamonn to promise to love her forever. His response was that he would love her until the Liver Birds flew away. As they embraced, a cheeky seagull swooped down and snatched a chip. The couple laughed at the spectacle and so did an old vagrant, who was standing on the landing stage, eyeing them wistfully.

Later that day, Rebecca noticed the framed photograph of a girl on the bedroom wall and she naturally asked Eamonn about her. At first, he claimed she was another of his cousins, then confessed that she was someone he had been going steady with, until a few months back. When Rebecca pressed him for the girl's name, Eamonn said it didn't matter and he removed the photograph and put it away in a drawer.

Over the next few days, the couple became very close but it also became evident that the Liverpudlian was trying to conceal something. Rebecca guessed it had something to do with the girl in the photograph, because each time she quizzed Eamonn about her, he would become irritated. He also became visibly nervous whenever anybody called at the flat, especially his friend Billy. The second time Billy turned up, he was slightly drunk and sneeringly claimed that Eamonn was not twenty-one, as he had told Rebecca, but twenty-nine. After that revelation Eamonn tried to push him out of the flat but Billy put up a fight and revealed another, even harsher truth, about his friend when he told the stunned Rebecca that he had a wife and two-year-old daughter in the Dingle area of Liverpool. Eamonn screamed at Billy to get out and punched him in the face. Billy's nose dripped with blood as he fled from the flat, threatening to return with his brothers.

At this point, the devastated Rebecca was in tears but she received no solace from Eamonn. On the contrary, he told her starkly,

'It's in the open now. Anyway, I don't love you, Becky. I just felt sorry for you. You're just a kid to me. You'd better leave. I'll pay for your fare home.'

She was so hurt by his callous words and attitude, that she just wanted to die. Numbly, she put on her coat and refused to take the fare.

'Where are you going?' Eamonn asked as he watched the broken-hearted teenager walk down the outside landing with her head bowed. He followed her down the stairs but when she reached the bottom she gave him the slip and ran off.

She wandered the unfamiliar city streets as the wintry gloom of evening descended. Snowflakes fell in whirling eddies and the raw, knife-edged wind from the river cut through her, adding to her misery. An hour later, at 10pm, she found herself on the deserted landing stage, gazing out across the Mersey. Warm tears dripped down her frozen cheeks as she decided on an agonizing death from her broken heart. She reminisced about the first time she had stood there, hand-in-hand with Eamonn and sadly recalled all the promises they'd made to each other on New Year's Day; how he'd love her until the Liver Birds flew away. Now it all meant nothing. As she stepped over the chains and prepared to jump, she replayed Eamonn's hurtful words over in her mind,

'I don't love you Becky, I just felt sorry for you.'

Half-blinded by the heavy flurry of crisp snowflakes and the sharp vortices of wind from the river, Rebecca took one step off the landing stage, ready to plunge into the dark swirling waters. She thought about the date of her death as she braced herself: Sunday, January 6th – Twelfth Night.

She screamed with shock as something powerful lifted her from under her arms. It felt like a strong pair of invisible hands. She was suddenly moving upwards and backwards over the landing stage and felt a churning in the pit of her stomach, as she sailed through the air. She came down in the middle of the landing stage and her feet hit the snow-covered wooden boards with a gentle thud. The girl was understandably perplexed and she spun round to find out who, or what, had miraculously saved her from plunging into the icy river.

There stood the white-haired vagrant who had been on the landing stage on New Year's Day. Rebecca was naturally afraid of the man and didn't know whether to thank him or flee from him.

With an expressionless look, he suddenly said:

'Those love too much who would die for love. Go home to your family tonight.' His voice had an eerie but refined quality, quite unlike any accent Rebecca had ever heard.

Sensing that there was something unearthly about the stranger, Rebecca backed away and ran from the landing stage. She bolted up the walkway, only glancing back once. Somehow, she wasn't surprised to find that he had vanished. Stranger still, upon that fateful Twelfth Night, she found a crisp, brand-new pound note in her coat pocket. At first, she surmised that Eamonn had slipped it in her coat but later became convinced that it was from the stranger on the landing stage.

She boarded the train back to Runcorn and gradually got over her disastrous adolescent crush.She later moved to London to work as a nurse in St Thomas's Hospital and married a paediatrician and bore him four children. To this day, Rebecca Bramley believes that the stranger on the landing stage who saved her life on that freezing Twelfth Night was an angel in disguise. At the very hour when the supernatural incident was taking place, Rebecca's mother, who wasn't a particularly religious woman, went into her bedroom and prayed to God for her daughter's safe return. Moments later, she felt a hand pat her shoulder reassuringly. Mrs Bramley was then overwhelmed with a warm sensation of peace and she somehow knew that Rebecca would soon return home safely.

According to the Bible, in Hebrews, it is written:

'Be not forgetful to entertain strangers, for thereby some have entertained angels unawares.'

Dreams that come true

At the very hour when the Titanic went down, a woman in New York awoke from a nightmare in which she had seen her mother in a crowded lifeboat in mid-ocean. In the nightmare, the dreamer could see hundreds of people in the icy waters crying out in agony as they drowned and, in the background, the ominous silhouette of the upturned liner's stern jutting out of the water, against a star-speckled sky. The dreamer later learned that her mother had indeed booked a passage on the ill-fated liner and had also been one of the lucky passengers who had been allowed onto the lifeboats.

Throughout the history of the human race, people have experienced dreams that seemed to reveal the future. As far back as 1450 BC, the Pharaoh Thutmose IV had a dream in which the spirit of the god, Hormakhu, asked him to clear away sand which had almost buried the Sphinx dedicated to him. In return for the deed, Hormakhu promised the pharaoh a long and fruitful reign. Thutmose cleared the sand away from Hormakhu's Sphinx and did, indeed, enjoy a long and prosperous reign. The pharaoh even had the dream engraved on a stone tablet, which was erected in front of the Great Sphinx of Giza.

Prophetic dreams seem to imply that, in the sleeping state, we prisoners of the present can somehow breach the barriers of time and space. Here are a couple of these fascinating, though often disturbing, dreams.

Almost every night for three weeks in March 1995, Jill, a Neston housewife, repeatedly encountered the same stranger in her dreams. He was a muscular young man, aged about twenty-five to thirty, with long red hair tied into a pony tail and a goatee beard. Jill knew no one of this description but her sceptical husband suggested that she had probably seen the character on TV.

At the end of that month, her husband was walking up the garden path on his return from work, when he suddenly dropped dead from heart failure. A week later, Jill stood sobbing at the graveside, as his coffin was lowered into the earth. Friends and relatives surrounded her, hugging and patting her, as she turned to walk from the grave. As the mourners headed for the funeral limousines, Jill turned to look back at the grave and there was the red-haired man, who had haunted her dreams over the past three weeks. He was one of the two grave-diggers who were ready to shovel the earth back over her husband's coffin. She almost fainted when she recognized his face, as he looked exactly as he had appeared in her dreams. In the years that have elapsed since that eerie incident, Jill has frequently wondered why she was given such a morbid preview of a person who would later feature in the darkest period of her life.

Another dream which foretold death, took place in the summer of 1981. Janet, a 28-year-old barmaid, met a 45-year-old chartered accountant named Steve Foster, at a pub in the Simm's Cross area of Widnes. Despite their age difference, they got on well and Janet arranged to see him again the following week. She told friends that she had finally met her Mr Right and couldn't wait to see him again. However, on the night before she was due to meet Steve, she had a disturbing dream, which she later recounted to her sister. She dreamt she was walking around with a black transparent veil draped over her head. In the dream, she saw her sister, Jackie, sobbing and, when she asked her what she was crying about, got no answer. The next part of the gloomy dream was deeply unsettling and surreal. Janet was paralysed and looking into a cracked mirror. In the reflection, she could see blood dribbling from her nostril and her front teeth were missing. She desperately wanted to scream but couldn't move an inch

On the following day, Steve collected Janet in his car and took her to his house in Runcorn. As the car was passing Runcorn Hill, a stray dog wandered into their path and Steve automatically swerved to avoid the animal. He lost control of the vehicle and crashed into railings. Janet had forgotten to fasten her seatbelt and she was catapulted through the windscreen. She hit the railings head-first and broke her neck, probably dying instantly. Steve staggered from the car in a daze and knelt beside her. Blood was trickling from her nose and her front teeth were missing. He placed his hand on her chest but could not detect a heartbeat. In a state of shock, he retrieved the wing mirror from his crashed car which was laying on the ground and held it over Janet's face, to see if it misted over from her breath. He had seen this done in countless movies and he anxiously inspected the cracked mirror but found no trace of mist.

When Jackie later told Steve about Janet's weird dream, he broke down and cried, realising that she had seen a vision of the fate which was to befall her.